HANDBOOK ON LEGAL METHODOLOGY

HANDBOOK ON LEGAL METHODOLOGY

From Objective to Method

Lina Kestemont

intersentia
Cambridge – Antwerp – Portland

Intersentia Ltd
Sheraton House | Castle Park
Cambridge | CB3 0AX | United Kingdom
Tel.: +44 1223 370 170 | Fax: +44 1223 370 169
Email: mail@intersentia.co.uk
www.intersentia.com | www.intersentia.co.uk

Distribution for the UK and Ireland:
NBN International
Airport Business Centre, 10 Thornbury Road
Plymouth, PL6 7 PP
United Kingdom
Tel.: +44 1752 202 301 | Fax: +44 1752 202 331
Email: orders@nbninternational.com

Distribution for Europe and all other countries:
Intersentia Publishing nv
Groenstraat 31
2640 Mortsel
Belgium
Tel.: +32 3 680 15 50 | Fax: +32 3 658 71 21
Email: mail@intersentia.be

Distribution for the USA and Canada:
International Specialized Book Services
920 NE 58th Ave. Suite 300
Portland, OR 97213
USA
Tel.: +1 800 944 6190 (toll free) | Fax: +1 503 280 8832
Email: info@isbs.com

Handbook on Legal Methodology. From Objective to Method

Cover image: "Parking Lot" by Bram Tack
A parking lot is an intriguing place to observe: cars come in from different angles and leave in different directions, all depending on the objectives of the drivers and their passengers. The same is true for researchers, as every research starts from a specific angle, develops its own methodology and follows its own course, all depending on the research's objectives.

ISBN 978-1-78068-673-8
D/2018/7849/42
NUR 820

British Library Cataloguing in Publication Data. A catalogue record for this book is available from the British Library.

For my parents, Hilde and René

To my daughter, Hanne

With special thanks to my husband, Bram

FOREWORD

The present book explores prevailing theories on the nature of legal science and legal methodology, and investigates its unique characteristics. In doing so, the book aims to enrich the burgeoning research on methodology of law with new insights, and tilts the methodology debate onto a new, concrete and practical level.

This book is meant to assist master students and PhD students in law to enter into the opaque and complex field of legal methodology, and to develop their own methodological skills. The approach is very hands-on and written with special attention for scholars carrying out legal research. Although the subject matter is one of the most challenging in legal literature, the book is easy to read and invites academics to use it in research practice or research instruction. Probably more than any other publication on the topic it brings theory and practice on research skills swiftly together. This book is also of relevance to funding agencies and policy makers. Understanding theory and practice of legal methodology is of utmost importance in the context of interdisciplinary research. There is a clear need to understand the particular features of legal methodology, as compared to methodologies applied in other social sciences. All in all, the book is strongly recommended for all those wo are in need of a hands-on manual on how to embark upon legal research, but at the same time tickles the interest of all those who show interest in research methodology at large.

The author, Lina Kestemont, stood out among other researchers at the Faculty of Law of the University of Leuven. It was crystal clear from the beginning in 2012 that she was as a very intelligent, ambitious and mature researcher, who showed a vigorous eagerness to explore a territory which was yet unknown to her: the area of methodology of law. She greedily joined our venture to strengthen legal methodology in the law curriculum by embracing the chance to assist in teaching legal methodology. Her input turned out to be vital in giving shape to our classes on legal methodology. The collaboration with Lina proved that she has the plasticity of mind and that she disposes over ample creativity and robustness to explore prevailing theories and assumptions in the field of methodology of law, and is able to guide research master and PhD students in law in their attempt to make their legal methodology explicit. Over the years we came to know Lina better, and realized even more how blessed we were having her around. Lina assumed leadership in the Research Master

Program without giving it a second thought, and lent her insights to set up a Crash Course Methodology for PhD students at our faculty. She was always keen to help research master students and to assist PhD students and professors in any way she could. The book very well reflects Lina's pedagogical attitude towards explaining research methodology. Lina is not the person to restrict her knowledge to mere theoretical considerations on legal research methodology. She wants to share her knowledge with fellow researchers and does it in a very accessible manner. By moments one can even feel the sheer enthusiasm that is typical to Lina's teaching approach.

We consider the author a top-notch scholar on legal methodology, an excellent teacher and a dear friend. Her intellectual strength and generous spirit will continue to inspire us.

Prof. dr. Paul Schoukens & Prof. dr. Geertrui Van Overwalle
University of Leuven, Belgium

WORDS OF GRATITUDE

This handbook is the result of a PhD project (2011–2016) for which I would like to thank several people. First of all, my supervisor Prof Dr Paul Schoukens. He was an excellent mentor who took the time to critically reflect on the project, to proofread my texts and to give feedback. He always stimulated me to seize chances, to improve my skills and to gain the necessary experience. His time and efforts made me a better scholar. I'm also grateful to my co-supervisor, Prof Dr Danny Pieters. He mentored me during my master years, gave me a warm welcome at the *Institute of Social Law* and learned me the basics of good legal research. Being offered a PhD position under his co-supervision was a great honour to me.

I would like to thank the members of my jury: Em Prof Dr Frank Hutsebaut (president), Prof Dr Geertrui Van Overwalle, Prof Dr Jeroen Maesschalck and Prof Dr Rob van Gestel. They all have supported and motivated me in their own way throughout my PhD project. In particular, I would like to thank Geertrui Van Overwalle for her mentorship during my years as a master and a PhD student. She taught me how to be critical and focused when analysing problems. Our meetings and conversations did not only improve my professionals skills, but also my confidence as a young, female scholar.

I am thankful for the support of my colleagues, in particular: Eleni, for her support in good times and bad, Carla, for all the practicalities, Karen to revise my texts and Kirsten for being there. I am also grateful to Els Vandensande, a colleague but most of all a friend who was my help and stay throughout the entire project.

I would like to thank my family for their continuous support: my siblings, Britta and Mike, their partners, Rien and Lore and my in-laws, the Tack family. I am very grateful to my father René who was prepared to proofread my texts at any time and my mother Hilde who in difficult times was always there to comfort me.

My final words of gratitude go to my husband, Bram. Writing a PhD is both an enriching and exhausting process, with many ups and downs. His loyal support throughout these five years was a sign of unconditional love and strong faith in my abilities; a gift for which I am truly grateful and of which I am reminded every day in our little girl, Hanne.

CONTENTS

1 INTRODUCTION

"La recherche en droit ou sur le droit n'est pas en quête de méthodes, mais elle est en quête d'identité quant à ses méthodes."[1]

1.1 NEED FOR AN EXPLICIT LEGAL METHODOLOGY

Legal scholarship is one of the oldest academic disciplines and the study of law has been passed on from generation to generation as an implicit *"savoir faire."*[2] This means that during their education legal students learned how to find, analyze, apply and improve the law without explicitly considering the methodological choices they make throughout this process.[3] Moreover, it was presumed that all legal scholars understood the methodology of legal research[4], making its explicit clarification and justification unnecessary.[5] Due to the absence of an explicit methodological tradition, handbooks and literature on legal methodology did not exist.[6] Therefore "the conventions, informal praxis, requirements and rules of play of academic legal research remain largely unwritten."[7]

The lack of an explicit legal methodology made it difficult for legal scholars to explain their research praxis to scholars from other academic disciplines.[8] The last decade this has become problematic because of the growing interdisciplinary collaboration at universities and the increased importance of external funding,

---

1 M. CUMYN and M. SAMSON, "La méthodologie juridique en quête d'identité", *RIEJ* 2013, 1.

2 S. PIMONT, "À propos de l'activité doctrinale civiliste", *RTD Civ.* 2006, 707.

3 H. TIJSSEN, *De juridische dissertatie onder de loep*, The Hague, Boom Juridische uitgevers, 2009, 145.

4 C. STOLKER, *Rethinking The Law School. Education, Research, Outreach and Governance*, Cambridge, Cambridge University Press, 2014, 204.

5 H. TIJSSEN, *De juridische dissertatie onder de loep*, The Hague, Boom Juridische uitgevers, 2009, 184.

6 H. TIJSSEN, *De juridische dissertatie onder de loep*, The Hague, Boom Juridische uitgevers, 2009, 168. The absence of literature on legal methodology was already mentioned by KUNNEMAN in 1986. F. KUNNEMAN, *Over het inleiden tot de rechtswetenschap*, Delft, Eburon, 1986, 26–27.

7 Translation of: "De conventies, informele praktijken, eisen en spelregels van rechtswetenschappelijk onderzoek zijn grotendeels ongeschreven [...]". J.B.M. VRANKEN, "Algemeen Deel. Een synthese" in *Mr. C. Assers Handleiding tot de beoefening van het Nederlands Burgerlijk Recht*, Deventer, Kluwer, 2014, 109. See also: C. STOLKER, *Rethinking The Law School. Education, Research, Outreach and Governance*, Cambridge, Cambridge University Press, 2014, 7.

8 See also: C. STOLKER, *Rethinking The Law School. Education, Research, Outreach and Governance*, Cambridge, Cambridge University Press, 2014, 224.

often granted by mixed experts panels.[9] Due to this, legal scholars have become more aware of the importance of an explicit methodology.

Despite an increased awareness[10], the reflection of legal scholars on methodology was too often limited to their own personal research experiences. Only occasionally the methodological identity of legal scholarship was studied from an empirical point of view.[11] In order to address this lacuna, a PhD project was designed to empirically explore the methodological features of legal scholarship. Essential to the project was a meta-methodological study of 45 Dutch-language PhDs on social security law defended at a Flemish or Dutch Law Faculty between 1971 and 2015. The results of the meta-study were used to complete and refine the existing, but limited literature on legal methodology.

The PhD project aimed to design an explicit methodological framework for legal scholarship. Such methodological framework lists on the one hand the *research objectives* legal scholars can pursue in their research, and on the other hand *their methodological features*. In this handbook we will discuss the developed methodological framework and provide legal scholars with a practical guide for designing their own research projects.

1.2 BASIC PRINCIPLES OF THE HANDBOOK

1.2.1 IMPORTANCE OF AN EXPLICIT METHODOLOGY

This handbook stresses the importance of an *explicit* research methodology. First of all, every methodological choice that researchers make does not only influence the research process, but also its results. It is therefore the responsibility of

---

9 R. VAN GESTEL and J. VRANKEN, "Assessing Legal Research: Sense and Nonsense of Peer Review versus Bibliometrics and the Need for a European Approach", *German Law Journal* 2011, 906; J.M. SMITS, *The Mind and Method of the Legal Academic*, Cheltenham, Edward Elgar, 2012, 109; C. STOLKER, *Rethinking The Law School. Education, Research, Outreach and Governance*, Cambridge, Cambridge University Press, 2014, 223–224.

10 See for example the so-called 'methodology debate' in The Netherlands, (re)inforced by STOLKER's *dies natalis* speech in 2003: *"Ja, geléérd zijn jullie wel! Over de status van de rechtswetenschap"*, Leiden University, 7 February 2003: https://openaccess.leidenuniv.nl/bitstream/handle/1887/3727/6_174_007.pdf?sequence=1.

11 H. TIJSSEN, *De juridische dissertatie onder de loep*, The Hague, Boom Juridische uitgevers, 2009, 252 p.; T. HUTCHINSON and N. DUNCAN, "Defining and describing what we do: Doctrinal Legal Research", *Deakin LR* 2012, 99; R.A.J. VAN GESTEL AND J.B.M., VRANKEN, "Rechtswetenschappelijke artikelen", *NJB* 2007, 1448–1461; E. BREMS, "Methods in Legal Human Rights Research" in COOMANS, F., GRÜNFELD, F. and KAMMINGA, T., *Methods of Human Rights Research*, Antwerp, Intersentia, 2009, 77–90; G., VAN DIJCK, *Kwaliteit van de juridische annotatie*, The Hague, Boom Juridische uitgevers, 2011, 170 p.; H. OOST, M. BREKELMANS, P. SWANBORN, & G. WESTHOFF, "Naar een didactiek van de probleemstelling", *Pedagogische Studiën Jaargang* 2002, 18–36.

legal scholars to clarify and justify their methodological choices.[12] Moreover, knowledge on the methodological underpinnings of a research allows for colleagues to verify and evaluate it.[13] They will be able to check whether the research questions were answered in a competent and independent way and on the basis of an adequate methodology.[14]

Second of all, a clarification of the researcher's starting points, assumptions and even expectations avoids "the risk of subjective colouring" and contributes to the transparency and reliability of the research.[15] This is of course beneficial to the quality of the research.[16] Although methodological explicitness does not as such guarantee high-quality research, it significantly reduces the risk of mistakes, incompleteness and bias.[17]

Finally, considering methodology in advance, i.e. prior to the actual research process, brings focus to research. The importance of a strong focus cannot be underestimated as it will define the research[18] and increase its feasibility. It allows for researchers to draft a "roadmap" which will keep them on the right track during the research process and make them ignore irrelevant sidetracks.[19] This will serve the efficiency of the research in terms of time, money and energy.[20]

---

12 M. BARENDRECHT, J. VRANKEN, I. GIESEN, M.J. BORGERS, W. VAN DER BURG, H.E.B. TIJSSEN, G.C.G.J. VAN ROERMUND and W.H. VAN BOOM, "Methoden van rechtswetenschap: komen we verder?", *NJB* 2004, 1423; N. HOEKX, K. VANHOVE and A. VERBEKE, "Yes we care! Bedenkingen over de (methode der) rechtswetenschap", *RW* 2008–09, 1787; H. TIJSSEN, *De juridische dissertatie onder de loep*, The Hague, Boom Juridische uitgevers, 2009, 43.

13 H. TIJSSEN, *De juridische dissertatie onder de loep*, The Hague, Boom Juridische uitgevers, 2009, 43 and references; N. HOEKX, K. VANHOVE and A. VERBEKE, "Yes we care! Bedenkingen over de (methode der) rechtswetenschap", *RW* 2008–09, 1787; B. VANGEEBERGEN and D. VAN DAELE, "Is de studie van het recht een wetenschap en wie kan het wat schelen?, *RW* 2009, 993; M. HERWEIJER, "Juridisch onderzoek" in J.W.L. BROEKSTEEG and E.F. STAMHUIS (eds.), *Rechtswetenschappelijk onderzoek. Over object en methode*, The Hague, Boom Juridische uitgevers, 2003, 27.

14 G.A.F.M. VAN SCHAAIJK, *Praktijkgericht juridisch onderzoek*, The Hague, Boom Juridische uitgevers, 2011, 35; B. VANGEEBERGEN and D. VAN DAELE, "Is de studie van het recht een wetenschap en wie kan het wat schelen?, *RW* 2009, 993.

15 Translation of: "het risico op subjectieve inkleuring" G.A.F.M. VAN SCHAAIJK, *Praktijkgericht juridisch onderzoek*, The Hague, Boom Juridische uitgevers, 2011, 36.

16 J.M. SMITS, *The Mind and Method of the Legal Academic*, Cheltenham, Edward Elgar, 2012, 180 p.

17 R.A.J. VAN GESTEL and J.B.M. VRANKEN, "Rechtswetenschappelijke artikelen", *NJB* 2007, 1460. See also TIJSSEN referring to a research of OOST and SONNEVELD (2004–2006) showing that an elaborated methodology contributes to the quality of a research. H. TIJSSEN, *De juridische dissertatie onder de loep*, The Hague, Boom Juridische uitgevers, 2009, 35.

18 B. VANGEEBERGEN and D. VAN DAELE, "Is de studie van het recht een wetenschap en wie kan het wat schelen?, *RW* 2009, 993.

19 R. VAN GESTEL, H.-W. MICKLITZ and M. POIARES MADURO, "Methodology in the New Legal World", *Department of Law EUI Working Papers*, 2012/13, 7.

20 See TIJSSEN referring to a research of OOST and SONNEVELD (2004–2006). H. TIJSSEN, *De juridische dissertatie onder de loep*, The Hague, Boom Juridische uitgevers, 2009, 35.

1.2.2 INDISPENSABLE LINK BETWEEN RESEARCH OBJECTIVE AND METHODOLOGICAL FEATURES

This handbook supports the principle that when deciding on their methodology legal scholars do not have a 'carte blanche' as there is an indispensable link between the type of research objective and its methodological features.[21] In this respect, ADAMS and GRIFFITHS aptly clarify that "questions go before methods, and until one has specified what the question is, no sensible discussion of methodology is possible."[22] After all, a description asks for a different methodology than an evaluation. Legal scholars who are not able to distinguish between their different types of research objectives run the risk of applying an inappropriate research methodology.[23]

Because of the indispensable link between the type of objective and its methodological features, we will address each research objective individually in this handbook. We distinguish between the descriptive, classifying, comparative, theory-building, explanatory, evaluative and recommendatory research objective.

1.2.3 RESULT OF A PHD PROJECT AT KU LEUVEN LAW FACULTY (2016)

This handbook on legal methodology was drafted on the basis of the results of a PhD project carried out at KU Leuven Law Faculty between 2011 and 2016.[24]

---

21 H. TIJSSEN, *De juridische dissertatie onder de loep*, The Hague, Boom Juridische uitgevers, 2009, 173; D. FELDMAN, "The Nature of Legal Scholarship", *The Modern Law Review* 1989, 503; E. FISHER, B. LANGE, E. SCOTFORD and C. CARLARNE, "Maturity and Methodology: Starting a Debate about Environmental Law Scholarship", *JEL* 2009, 244; N. HOEKX, K. VANHOVE and A. VERBEKE, "Yes we care! Bedenkingen over de (methode der) rechtswetenschap", *RW* 2008–09, 1787; J.M. SMITS, *The Mind and Method of the Legal Academic*, Cheltenham, Edward Elgar, 2012, 34 & 119; M. HERWEIJER, "Juridisch onderzoek" in J.W.L. BROEKSTEEG and E.F. STAMHUIS (eds.), *Rechtswetenschappelijk onderzoek. Over object en methode*, The Hague, Boom Juridische uitgevers, 2003, 28; M. SALTER and J. MASON, *Writing Law Dissertations*, Essex, Pearson, 2007, 109; M. ADAMS, "Doing What Doesn't Come Naturally. On the Distinctiveness of Comparative Law," in M. VAN HOECKE (ed.), *Methodologies of Legal Research*, Oxford, Hart Publishing, 2011, 236; R. CRYER, T. HERVEY and B. SOKHI-BULLEY, *Research Methodologies in EU and International Law*, Oxford, Hart Publishing, 2011, 8; B. VANGEEBERGEN and D. VAN DAELE, "Is de studie van het recht een wetenschap en wie kan het wat schelen?, *RW* 2009, 992–993; M.H. WISSINK, "Op weg naar een nieuwe ronde", *NJB* 2006, 1365; M. VAN HOECKE, "Preface" in M. VAN HOECKE (ed.), *Methodologies of Legal Research*, Oxford, Hart Publishing, 2011, viii; J. HAGE, "The Method of a Truly Normative Legal Science" in M. VAN HOECKE (ed.), *Methodologies of Legal Research*, Oxford, Hart Publishing, 2011, 23; C. MORRIS and C. MURPHY, *Getting a PhD in Law*, Oxford, Hart Publishing, 2011, 38–39.

22 M. ADAMS and J. GRIFFITHS, "Against 'comparative method': explaining similarities and differences" in M. ADAMS and J. BOMHOFF (eds.), *Practice and Theory in Comparative Law*, Cambridge, Cambridge University Press, 2012, 279.

23 G. DE GEEST, "Hoe maken we van de rechtswetenschap een volwaardige wetenschap?", *NJB* 2004, 58.

24 L. KESTEMONT, *Naar een rechtswetenschappelijke methodeleer. Een expliciet methodologisch kader voor rechtswetenschappelijk onderzoek in het socialezekerheidsrecht*, Public defence:

As previously mentioned, the PhD project aimed to empirically explore the methodology of legal research in order to design an explicit methodological framework. The project consisted of three parts: (i) drafting a typology on 'research objectives and their methodological features' on the basis of a profound literature study, (ii) conducting a meta-methodological study on existing legal research, and (iii) confronting the typology with the results of the meta-study in order to establish an explicit methodological framework.

As with every research also this PhD project had its limits. First of all, the project focused on what we call *traditional legal research* having as object of study "applicable law, as laid down in written and unwritten national, European or international rules, principles, concepts, doctrines and case law, and as commented on in literature."[25] A traditional legal research studies law from an internal-legal perspective, rather than as a social or cultural phenomenon.[26] Because of its focus on traditional legal research, the PhD project – and therefore also this handbook – largely left out multi- or interdisciplinary research in which legal scholars apply "assumptions, paradigms, methods, theories, concepts, etc." from other academic disciplines.[27] In the handbook we do, however, indicate when a traditional legal research is likely to transform into a multi- or interdisciplinary research.

Second of all, although the praxis of searching, selecting, analyzing and synthesizing sources forms an inherent part of legal research, it is an area of study in itself which was not dealt with in the PhD project.[28] Specific guidelines on how to deal with legal sources will therefore not be discussed in this handbook.

Third of all, literature which explicitly focuses on the objectives and methodological features of legal scholarship is rather rare.[29] Standard works or

Leuven, 16th of September 2016, prof. dr. P. Schoukens (supervisor), prof. dr. D. Pieters (co-supervisor), published in 2017 by die Keure (Bruges) in the Begasoz/ Abetrass series. In July 2017, the dissertation won the three-yearly Walter Leën Prize.

25 Translation of: "heeft als object het geldende positief recht zoals dat is neergelegd in geschreven en ongeschreven nationale, Europese of internationale regels, beginselen, begrippen, leerstukken en rechterlijke uitspraken, en van commentaar voorzien in de literatuur." J.B.M. VRANKEN, "Algemeen Deel. Een synthese" in *Mr. C. Assers Handleiding tot de beoefening van het Nederlands Burgerlijk Recht*, Deventer, Kluwer, 2014, 6.

26 C. STOLKER, *Rethinking The Law School. Education, Research, Outreach and Governance*, Cambridge, Cambridge University Press, 2014, 114.

27 Translation of: "vooronderstellingen, paradigma's, methoden, theorieën, begrippen en dergelijke". J.B.M. VRANKEN, "Algemeen Deel. Een synthese" in *Mr. C. Assers Handleiding tot de beoefening van het Nederlands Burgerlijk Recht*, Deventer, Kluwer, 2014, 182–183.

28 See for example: J.B.M. VRANKEN, "Algemeen Deel. Een synthese" in *Mr. C. Assers Handleiding tot de beoefening van het Nederlands Burgerlijk Recht*, Deventer, Kluwer, 2014, 234 p.; M.V.R. SNEL, "Source-usage within doctrinal legal inquiry: choices, problems, and challenges", *ReM* 2014, afl. 3, 21 p. and SNEL's PhD thesis "Meester(s) over bronnen" defended at Tilburg University in 2016.

29 See also: R. VAN GESTEL, H.-W. MICKLITZ and M. POIARES MADURO, "Methodology in the New Legal World", *Department of Law EUI Working Papers*, 2012/13, 20; R.C.P. HAENTJENS, C. HELLINGMAN, O.W.M. KAMSTRA, F.B.M. KUNNEMAN and M. VERHORST, "Object en methode in de Nederlandse rechtswetenschap: op zoek naar standpunten", *NJB* 1985, 807.

handbooks are lacking and authors tackle the topic mostly indirectly, without an in-depth discussion (with the exception of methods for comparative law and interpretation). As point of departure for the literature study – which was at the basis of the first part of the PhD project – we therefore opted for the contributions written in light of the 'Dutch methodology debate'[30] and afterwards applied the so-called *snowball method* in order to find other relevant contributions.[31] Literature from common law traditions was approached with some prudence as many authors alert to the differences between civil law and common law research.[32]

Finally, the meta-methodological study of the PhD project was confined to 45 Dutch-language PhDs on social security law defended at a Flemish or Dutch Law Faculty between 1971 and 2015. The choice to study PhDs was motivated by the fact that their 'academic' status is undisputed (contrary to some other legal publications, such as annotations or overviews of jurisprudence). Next, we decided to look at PhDs written in the field of social security law as it concerns a relatively young legal discipline which has significantly developed over the last decennia. However, the number of PhDs written in this field were manageable and therefore constituted a feasible dataset for the meta-study. Finally, only Dutch-language PhDs were included. As a meta-methodological study is of an intrinsic interpretative nature[33], the correct interpretation of the written PhDs, regardless of their different linguistic usage, vocabulary and style of writing, was

---

30 (Re)inforced by STOLKER's *dies natalis* speech at Leiden University in 2003: *"Ja, geléérd zijn jullie wel! Over de status van de rechtswetenschap"*, Leiden University, 7 February 2003: https://openaccess.leidenuniv.nl/bitstream/handle/1887/3727/6_174_007.pdf?sequence=1.

31 G.A.F.M. VAN SCHAAIJK, *Praktijkgericht juridisch onderzoek*, The Hague, Boom Juridische uitgevers, 2011, 116.

32 Firstly, the role of legislation and precedents strongly differs from civil to common law traditions. (R. VAN GESTEL and H.-W. MICKLITZ, "Revitalising Doctrinal Legal Research in Europe: What About Methodology?" in U. NEERGAARD, R. NIELSEN and L. ROSEBERRY (eds.), *European Legal Method – Paradoxes and Revitalisation*, Kopenhagen, DJØF Publishing, 2011, 65.) Secondly, common law researchers spend a lot of attention to the facts of legal cases, whereas civil law researchers tend to quicker leave the facts behind in order to look for underlying principles. (K. LEMMENS, "Comparative law as an act of modesty: a pragmatic and realistic approach to comparative legal scholarship" in M. ADAMS and J. BOMHOFF (eds.), *Practice and Theory in Comparative Law*, Cambridge, Cambridge University Press, 2012, 319.) Thirdly, "common law is said to be inductive, pragmatic, fact-bound, and past-oriented, the civil law is deductive, logical and systematic, rule-bound, and future-oriented." (M.M. SIEMS, "A World without Law Professors" in M. VAN HOECKE (ed.), *Methodologies of Legal Research*, Oxford, Hart Publishing, 2011, 75.) And finally, legal research in civil law countries tends to be more of a traditional nature, whereas in the UK *socio-legal studies* and in the US *law and economics* and *empirical legal studies* have grown considerably. C. STOLKER, *Rethinking The Law School. Education, Research, Outreach and Governance*, Cambridge, Cambridge University Press, 2014, 211; R. VAN GESTEL, "Evaluating Legal Research; About the Good, the Bad, and the Ugly" in T. TANQUEREL and A. FLÜKIGER (eds.), *L'évaluation de la recherche en droit. Enjeux et méthodes*, Bruylant, Brussels, 2015, 54; M. VAN HOECKE, "De evaluatie van rechtswetenschappelijk onderzoek", *RW* 2015, 139).

33 B.L., PATTERSON, S.E., THORNE, C., CANAM and C., JILLINGS, *Meta-Study of Qualitative Health Research*, Thousand Oaks, Sage, 2001, 74.

essential. The choice for PhDs in our mother tongue (Dutch) can therefore be considered as a precautionary measure in view of the interpretative nature of the meta-study. The Dutch-language PhDs were searched for at both Dutch and Flemish law faculties, until June 2015. For more information on the search and selection of the PhDs or a more in-depth motivation of the dataset, we refer to the PhD project itself.[34]

1.3 STRUCTURE OF THE HANDBOOK

In the following, we will discuss the objectives and methodological features of legal research in a coherent and structured way.

First, we distinguish and clarify the different types of research objectives that legal scholars can pursue in their research: descriptive, classifying, comparative, theory-building, explanatory, evaluative and recommendatory.

Second, as each type of research objective calls for its own methodology, we discuss the methodological features of each type of research objective individually.

Third, after looking into each research objective separately, we will address three overall methodological features applicable to all research objectives. They concern: the importance of dissent, the interactions which can arise between different types of research objectives and the researcher's *frame of reference*.

Finally, we conclude by transforming the theory of the previous parts into a practical methodological guide for legal research. This guide serves as a useful instrument for legal scholars who aim to design or reflect on their own research project.

---

[34] L. KESTEMONT, *Naar een rechtswetenschappelijke methodeleer. Een expliciet methodologisch kader voor rechtswetenschappelijk onderzoek in het socialezekerheidsrecht*, Bruges, die Keure, 2017, 100–104.

2 RESEARCH OBJECTIVES

Traditional legal research can pursue different types of research objectives. We distinguish between descriptive, classifying, comparative, theory-building, explanatory, evaluative and recommendatory research objectives.[1] The number and/or different types of research objectives always depend on the research itself: the topic of the research, its complexity, the available time, etc.

In what follows, each type of research objective will be discussed separately. During the research process different types of research objectives can, however, interact with each other. Part 4 of this book will discuss these possible interactions.

2.1 DESCRIPTIVE RESEARCH OBJECTIVE

Describing the law is the first step in any legal research.[2] "It is not a subordinate activity of the legal researcher, but concerns an essential constituent of his work: it is impossible to work on the law without assembling, ordering and describing it".[3] A descriptive research objective will therefore usually proceed the other objectives of a research, such as classifications, comparisons, evaluations etc. Describing the law can, however, also be the main and only objective of a legal research. In this case, the research focuses on retrieving the scope and meaning

1 The typology on research objectives was developed in our PhD project and previously discussed in the article: L. KESTEMONT, "A Meta-Methodological Study of Dutch and Belgian PhDs on Social Security Law: Devising a Typology Of Research Objectives as a Supporting Tool", *European Journal of Social Security* 2015, 361–384.

2 M. VAN HOECKE, "Aard en methode van de rechtsdogmatiek", *R & R* 1984, 191; C. STOLKER, *Rethinking The Law School. Education, Research, Outreach and Governance*, Cambridge, Cambridge University Press, 2014, 212.

3 Translation of: "Het gaat hier niet om een bijkomstige nevenwerkzaamheid van de rechtswetenschappelijke onderzoeker, maar om een essentieel bestanddeel van zijn werk: zonder verzameling, ordening en beschrijving van de rechtsstof kan men niet verder werken aan die rechtsstof." A.R. BLOEMBERGEN, "Iets over object en methode van wetenschap en rechtspraak in het privaatrecht" in O.W.M. KAMSTRA, F.B.M. KUNNEMAN & C.W. MARIS (eds.), *Nederlandse rechtswetenschap. Tussen distantie en betrokkenheid: paradigma's in de twintigste eeuw*, Zwolle, W.E.J. Tjeenk Willink, 1988, 74. See also: E.L. RUBIN, "The Practice and Discourse of Legal Scholarship", *Mich.L.Rev.* 1987–88, 1849; R.A.J. VAN GESTEL and J.B.M. VRANKEN, "Rechtswetenschappelijke artikelen", *NJB* 2007, 1454.

of a legal concept or construct.[4] As the law is constantly changing, it is an important task of legal scholars to describe its altered meaning and scope.[5]

According to TIJSSEN, "to describe means to map out. In order to understand a phenomenon it has to be analyzed, i.e. systematically dividing it into different parts. In a description something will be presented and explained in its different components."[6] This definition clarifies that a descriptive research objective aims to systematically analyze legal constructs in all their components in order to present them in an accurate, significant and orderly manner.[7]

Legal scholars often claim that a mere display or summary of existing law is not enough to qualify as academic legal research.[8] A legal researcher cannot simply re-describe existing knowledge, but should always add something to the existing body of knowledge.[9] This claim is true if the description of law is the main – and therefore only – objective of a research. However, in most legal research describing the law serves other objectives (e.g. comparisons or evaluations of law). In those cases the description of law is not necessarily 'original' or 'adding something new to the existing body of knowledge', as it most often concerns legislation, case law and legal doctrine already described by other scholars. Although these descriptions do not contribute as such to the existing body of knowledge, they are necessary for the further course of the research. Moreover, every legal research has its own scope and perspective, depending on the researcher, the topic, the sources, the main research

---

4 M. VAN HOECKE, *Is de rechtswetenschap een empirische wetenschap?*, The Hague, Boom Juridische uitgevers, 2010, 19.

5 M. VAN HOECKE, *Is de rechtswetenschap een empirische wetenschap?*, The Hague, Boom Juridische uitgevers, 2010, 38.

6 Translation of: "Beschrijven betekent in dit verband in kaart brengen. Om een verschijnsel te leren kennen zal het geanalyseerd moeten worden, d.w.z. op een systematische wijze in onderdelen verdelen. In een beschrijving wordt iets uiteengezet en uitgelegd uit welke delen het bestaat." (Referring to H. OOST and A. MARKENHOF, 2007). H. TIJSSEN, *De juridische dissertatie onder de loep*, The Hague, Boom Juridische uitgevers, 2009, 58. See also: G.A.F.M. VAN SCHAAIJK, *Praktijkgericht juridisch onderzoek*, The Hague, Boom Juridische uitgevers, 2011, 71.

7 H. OOST, *Circling Around a Question: Defining Your Research Problem*, IVLOS, Utrecht 2003, 34; H. TIJSSEN, *De juridische dissertatie onder de loep*, The Hague, Boom juridische uitgevers, 2009, 58; G.A.F.M. VAN SCHAAIJK, *Praktijkgericht juridisch onderzoek*, The Hague, Boom Juridische Uitgevers, 2011, 71; F. KUNNEMAN, *Rechtswetenschap*, Nijmegen, Ars Aequi Libri, 1991, 5; A.M. HOL, "Pleidooi voor een jurisprudentia. Over recht en rechtswetenschap" in J.W.L. BROEKSTEEG and E.F. STAMHUIS (eds.), *Rechtswetenschappelijk onderzoek. Over object en methode*, The Hague, Boom Juridische Uitgevers, 2003, 10.

8 J.M. BARENDRECHT, "Rechtswetenschap: stoffig of inventief?", *NJB* 1996, 707; VLIR KWALITEITSZORG ONDERZOEK RECHTEN, *Model voor Integrale Kwaliteitsevaluatie van het Onderzoek in de Rechtswetenschappen*, versie 22 september 2004, www.vlir.be/media/docs/Onderzoeksbeleid/notitie_KZR_22sept2004.pdf, 14; J.M. SMITS, *The Mind and Method of the Legal Academic*, Cheltenham, Edward Elgar, 2012, 103.

9 N. HOEKX, K. VANHOVE and A. VERBEKE, "Yes we care! Bedenkingen over de (methode der) rechtswetenschap", *RW* 2008–09, 1787; J.M. BARENDRECHT, "Rechtswetenschap: stoffig of inventief?", *NJB* 1996, 708; R.A. POSNER, "Legal Scholarship Today", *Harv.L.Rev.* 2002, 1320; R.A.J VAN GESTEL, Preadvies "Kwaliteit van juridische publicaties. Over ranking, peer review, sciëntometrics en vertrouwen in alternatieve evaluatiemethoden" in HANDELINGEN NEDERLANDSE JURISTEN-VERENIGING, *Kwaliteit als keuze in rechtspraak, wetgeving en rechtswetenschap*, Deventer, Kluwer, 2015, 338.

objective and the limitations. Legal scholars will therefore never take over an existing description of law, but will always describe it from their own point of view.

2.2 CLASSIFYING RESEARCH OBJECTIVE

A classifying research objective aims to classify (legal) phenomena in the existing legal system.[10] This means that factual situations, court judgments and new regulations are ranged under existing legal doctrines (e.g. the doctrine on the abuse of the law), existing legal concepts (e.g. aleatory contracts) or existing legal constructs (e.g. tontines).[11] It is possible that a given phenomenon cannot be classified under an existing legal category, because of its unique characteristics. In that case a new legal category will arise.

Classification is a typical and essential objective of legal scholarship.[12] First of all, classifying a legal system does not only allow understanding the system and disseminating knowledge, but also working on it.[13] In other words, classification results in a meaningful, organized, accessible, understandable and workable legal system.[14] It allows determining which legal rules or principles are applicable to a particular situation.[15]

Second, classifying research objectives contribute to the further development and refinement of the legal system. In this respect, legal scholars can examine whether (new) social phenomena or factual situations – currently without their own regulating legal framework – can be classified under existing legal categories, as a result of which legal rules or principles become applicable.[16]

---

10 J.M. SMITS, *The Mind and Method of the Legal Academic*, Cheltenham, Edward Elgar, 2012, 18.

11 M. BARENDRECHT, J. VRANKEN, I. GIESEN, M.J. BORGERS, W. VAN DER BURG, H.E.B. TIJSSEN, G.C.G.J. VAN ROERMUND and W.H. VAN BOOM, "Methoden van rechtswetenschap: komen we verder?", *NJB* 2004, 1425; H. TIJSSEN, *De juridische dissertatie onder de loep*, The Hague, Boom Juridische uitgevers, 2009, 58 (refering to H. OOST & A. MARKENHOF, *Een onderzoek voorbereiden*, Baarn, HB-uitgevers, 2007); H. OOST, *Hoe schrijf ik een betere scriptie. Een nieuwe methode voor het schrijven van scripties en andere teksten*, Amsterdam, Contact, 1995, 45; J.M. POLAK, *Theorie en practijk der rechtsvinding*, Zwolle, W.E.J. Tjeenk Willink, 1953, 31–32.

12 M. VAN HOECKE, *Is de rechtswetenschap een empirische wetenschap?*, The Hague, Boom Juridische uitgevers, 2010, 13; A. AARNIO, *Denkweisen der Rechtswissenschaft*, Wien, Springer, 1979, 50; J.M. BARENDRECHT, "Rechtswetenschap: stoffig of inventief?", *NJB* 1996, 712; A. PECZENIK, "Scientia Juris. Legal Doctrine as knowledge of Law and as a Source of Law" in E. PATTARO (ed.), *A Treatise of Legal Philosopy and General Jurisprudence*, Dordrecht, Springer, 2005, 1; N. MACCORMICK, *Rhetoric and the Rule of* Law, Oxford, Oxford University Press, 2005, 3.

13 See also: G. SAMUEL, *Epistemology and Method in Law*, Aldershot, Ashgate, 2003, 217; P. SCHOLTEN, "Algemeen Deel" in *Asser's Handleiding tot de beoefening van het Nederlandsch Burgerlijk Recht*, Zwolle, W.E.J. Tjeenk Willink, 1954, 60.

14 See. F. KUNNEMAN, *Rechtswetenschap*, Nijmegen, Ars Aequi Libri, 1991, 7; R. KRANENBURG, *De grondslagen der rechtswetenschap*, Haarlem, Tjeenk Willink, 1952, 23.

15 N. MACCORMICK, *Rhetoric and the Rule of* Law, Oxford, Oxford University Press, 2005, 141.

16 P. WESTERMAN and M. WISSINK, "Rechtsgeleerdheid als rechtswetenschap", *NJB* 2008, 504.

Finally, at the beginning of a research legal scholars will often clarify the main concepts of their study or develop a conceptual framework.[17] Conceptualization is necessary as the scope or meaning of legal concepts is not always clear or undisputed, and can have an important effect on the scope of the research.[18] In order to define these concepts, legal scholars will have to classify them in terms of their role/purpose/function within the legal system and in terms of their relation with other legal concepts and categories. Conceptualization can therefore be qualified as a classifying research objective.[19]

2.3 COMPARATIVE RESEARCH OBJECTIVE

"Comparative Law is somewhat like traveling. The traveler and the comparatist are invited to break away from daily routines, to meet the unexpected and, perhaps, to get to know the unknown."[20]

A comparative research objective aims to compare two or more legal constructs in order to uncover their similarities and differences. In traditional legal research we distinguish between internal, historical and external comparison.

Internal comparison implies a comparison of legal concepts from the same legal system.[21] Such a comparison is possible within one legal discipline (e.g. to compare unemployment benefits of employees to those of civil servants) or between different legal disciplines (e.g. comparing the concept 'employee' in labour law to the same concept in social security law).[22] Finally, it is also possible to compare between different state levels: federal, regional and municipal law, or even between sectorial collective agreements.[23] So it may not be surprising that internal comparisons

17 L. KESTEMONT, *Naar een rechtswetenschappelijke methodeleer. Een expliciet methodologisch kader voor rechtswetenschappelijk onderzoek in het socialezekerheidsrecht*, Bruges, die Keure (reeks Begasoz/ Abetrass), 2017, 114.

18 L. KESTEMONT, *Naar een rechtswetenschappelijke methodeleer. Een expliciet methodologisch kader voor rechtswetenschappelijk onderzoek in het socialezekerheidsrecht*, Bruges, die Keure (series Begasoz/ Abetrass), 2017, 132.

19 L. KESTEMONT, *Naar een rechtswetenschappelijke methodeleer. Een expliciet methodologisch kader voor rechtswetenschappelijk onderzoek in het socialezekerheidsrecht*, Bruges, die Keure (series Begasoz/ Abetrass), 2017, 192.

20 G. FRANKENBERG, "Critical Comparisons: Re-thinking Comparative Law", *Harv.Int'l L.J.* 1985, 411–412.

21 W. DEVROE, *Rechtsvergelijking in een context van europeanisering en globalisering*, Leuven, Acco, 2010, 34–35; H. TIJSSEN, *De juridische dissertatie onder de loep*, The Hague, Boom juridische uitgevers, 2009, 76; M.H. WISSINK, "Op weg naar een nieuwe ronde", *NJB* 2006, 1363; A.E. ODERKERK, *De preliminaire fase van het rechtsvergelijkend onderzoek*, Nijmegen, Ars Aequi Libri, 1999, 5.

22 M. HERWEIJER, "Juridisch onderzoek" in J.W.L. BROEKSTEEG & E.F. STAMHUIS (eds.), *Rechtswetenschappelijk onderzoek. Over object en methode*, The Hague, Boom Juridische uitgevers, 2003, 31.

23 D. PIETERS, "Functions of comparative law and practical methodology of comparing" in *Syllabus Research Master in Law*, Leuven-Tilburg, 2009, 10.

can be rather diverse: comparing between (modalities of) regulations, groups of individuals, legal institutions, case law of different courts, etc.[24]

A *historical comparison* compares legal constructs from different periods in time. For example: how was Roman private law reflected in various legal systems? Did they have similar legal constructs?[25] Historical comparisons do not qualify as legal history, because the past is not approached diachronically. On the contrary, legal constructs from different periods in time are compared in a synchronic and static way.[26] When opting for a historical comparison, it is important to realize that in the past some problems or legal constructs did not (yet) exist or have developed over time. After all, law and societal developments are closely intertwined: for example, legislation to protect shareholders can only exist in a society with a capital market.[27]

An *external comparison* compares (legal constructs from) two or more legal systems.[28] These legal systems can be compared on a national, supranational or international level.[29] External comparison is quite popular in legal scholarship as it allows exceeding national boundaries. Its outcomes can lead to a classification of legal families, can be helpful or inspiring when trying to solve a national problem, can put one's own legal system into perspective and can even be essential when considering harmonization measures.[30]

---

24 L. KESTEMONT, *Naar een rechtswetenschappelijke methodeleer. Een expliciet methodologisch kader voor rechtswetenschappelijk onderzoek in het socialezekerheidsrecht*, Bruges, die Keure (series Begasoz/ Abetrass), 2017, 135–137.

25 Example from: M. LÖHNIG, "A Few Words about Comparative Legal History" in M. ADAMS & D. HEIRBAUT (eds.), *The Method and Culture of Comparative Law*, Oxford, Hart Publishing, 2014, 115.

26 D. PIETERS, "Functions of comparative law and practical methodology of comparing" in *Syllabus Research Master in Law*, Leuven-Tilburg, 2009, 11; W. DEVROE, *Rechtsvergelijking in een context van europeanisering en globalisering*, Leuven, Acco, 2010, 29; J. HUSA, "Research Designs of Comparative Law" in M. ADAMS and D. HEIRBAUT (eds.), *The Method and Methodology*, Oxford, Hart Publishing, 2014, 58.

27 R. MICHAELS, "The Functional Method of Comparative Law" in M. REIMANN and R. ZIMMERMANN (eds.), *The Oxford Handbook of Comparative Law*, Oxford, Oxford University Press, 2006, 368.

28 W. PINTENS, *Inleiding tot de rechtsvergelijking*, Leuven, Universitaire Pers Leuven, 1998, 16; A.E. ODERKERK, *De preliminaire fase van het rechtsvergelijkend onderzoek*, Nijmegen, Ars Aequi Libri, 1999, 5; W. DEVROE, *Rechtsvergelijking in een context van europeanisering en globalisering*, Leuven, Acco, 2010, 35; M. VAN HOECKE, *Is de rechtswetenschap een empirische wetenschap?*, The Hague, Boom Juridische uitgevers, 2010, 14; F. GORLÉ, G. BOURGEOIS, H. BOCKEN, F. REYNTJENS, W. DE BONDT & K. LEMMENS, *Rechtsvergelijking*, Mechelen, Kluwer, 2007, 1.

29 HUSA discusses *horizontal comparison* and *vertical comparison*. J. HUSA, "Research Designs of Comparative Law" in M. ADAMS & D. HEIRBAUT (eds.), *The Method and Methodology*, 2014, 59; D. PIETERS, "Functions of comparative law and practical methodology of comparing" in *Syllabus Research Master in Law*, Leuven-Tilburg, 2009, 10.

30 Compilation of: D. PIETERS, "Functions of comparative law and practical methodology of comparing" in *Syllabus Research Master in Law*, Leuven-Tilburg, 2009, 3 ff; G. DANNEMANN, "Comparative Law: Study of Similarities or Differences" in M. REIMANN and R. ZIMMERMANN (eds.), *The Oxford Handbook of Comparative Law*, Oxford, Oxford University Press, 2006, 401–406.; M. VAN HOECKE, "Deep Level Comparative Law" in M. VAN HOECKE (ed.), *Epistemology and Methodology of Comparative Law*, Oxford, Hart,

Although we distinguish three types of comparison, it is possible to combine them: for example, on the one hand comparing liability issues of employees in national public and private sectors *(internal)*, and on the other hand comparing liability schemes in three different EU member states (*external*).[31]

2.4 THEORY-BUILDING RESEARCH OBJECTIVE

"Theorizing involves trying to get a better understanding of particulars by seeing them in a more abstract and general way."[32]

A theory-building research objective aims to uncover patterns or common denominators from a set of legal rules or cases in order to develop a model or a theory.[33] Legal scholars do not often use the concepts 'theory' or 'model'; instead they refer to 'legal doctrines'.[34] Examples are the tort doctrine or the doctrine on the abuse of rights.[35] A theory-building research objective will in the end result

---

2004, 172; A.E. ODERKERK, *De preliminaire fase van het rechtsvergelijkend onderzoek*, Nijmegen, Ars Aequi Libri, 1999, 73–88; J. HILL, "Comparative Law, Law Reform and Legal Theory", *O.J.L.S.* 1989, 102; F. KUNNEMAN, *Rechtswetenschap*, Nijmegen, Ars Aequi Libri, 1991, 48; W. PINTENS, *Inleiding tot de rechtsvergelijking*, Leuven, Universitaire Pers Leuven, 1998, 33 ff.; W. DEVROE, *Rechtsvergelijking in een context van europeanisering en globalisering*, Leuven, Acco, 2010, 30–32; C. MORRIS and C. MURPHY, *Getting a PhD in Law*, Oxford, Hart Publishing, 2011, 37.

31 L. KESTEMONT, *Naar een rechtswetenschappelijke methodeleer. Een expliciet methodologisch kader voor rechtswetenschappelijk onderzoek in het socialezekerheidsrecht*, Bruges, die Keure (reeks Begasoz/ Abetrass), 2017, 135.

32 W. TWINING, *Law in context*, Oxford, Clarendon Press, 1997, 134.

33 P. SCHOLTEN, "De structuur der rechtswetenschap" in *Verzamelde Geschriften van wijlen Prof. Mr. Paul Scholten*, Zwolle, Tjeenk Willink, 1949, 401; P. SCHLAG, "Spam Jurisprudence, Air Law, and the Rank of Anxiety of Nothing Happening, *Geo.L.J.* 2009, 809; J.M. FEINMAN, "The Jurisprudence of Classification", *Stan.L.Rev.* 1989, 681; L. ALEXANDER, "What We Do, and Why We Do it", *Stan.L.Rev.* 1993, 1898. See also: COUNCIL OF AUSTRALIAN LAW DEANS, *Statement on the Nature of Legal Research*, May and October 2005, https://cald.asn.au/wp-content/uploads/2017/11/cald-statement-on-the-nature-of-legal-research-20051.pdf.

34 G. DE GEEST, "Hoe maken we van de rechtswetenschap een volwaardige wetenschap?", *NJB* 2004, 59; J.B.M. VRANKEN, "Algemeen Deel. Een synthese" in *Mr. C. Assers Handleiding tot de beoefening van het Nederlands Burgerlijk Recht*, Deventer, Kluwer, 2014, 50; A.R. BLOEMBERGEN, "Iets over object en methode van wetenschap en rechtspraak in het privaatrecht" in O.W.M. KAMSTRA, F.B.M. KUNNEMAN and C.W. MARIS (eds.), *Nederlandse rechtswetenschap. Tussen distantie en betrokkenheid: paradigma's in de twingtigste eeuw*, Zwolle, W.E.J. Tjeenk Willink, 1988, 73; G. VAN SCHAAIJK, "Praktijkgericht juridisch onderzoek", *ReM* 2011, afl. 1, 88; M. VAN HOECKE, *Is de rechtswetenschap een empirische wetenschap?*, The Hague, Boom Juridische uitgevers, 2010, 23.

35 M. VAN HOECKE, "Aard en methode van de rechtsdogmatiek", *R&R* 1984, 197; A. PECZENIK, "Scientia Juris. Legal Doctrine as knowledge of Law and as a Source of Law" in E. PATTARO (ed.), *A Treatise of Legal Philosopy and General Jurisprudence*, Dordrecht, Springer, 2005, 33; M. VAN QUICKENBORNE, "Rechtsstudie als wetenschap" in *Actori incumbit probatio. Opstellen aangeboden ter gelegenheid van de eerst promotie rechten aan de universitaire instelling Antwerpen*, Antwerp, Kluwer, 1975, 230.

in a new theory, an alteration or replacement of an old theory, or a reduction of two existing theories to one general theory.[36]

A legal theory is "a system of coherent, non-contradictory assertions, views and concepts concerning some legal system or part of it, which are worded in such a way that it is possible to deduct from them explanations or predictions concerning the validity or the functioning of legal concepts, rules or principles".[37] This definition clarifies that a theory has both a predictory and an explanatory function. For example, the doctrine on legitimate expectations will help to clarify whether or not an individual has to comply to a specific commitment in particular situation.[38] In this respect, a legal theory will always have an important practical applicability.[39]

Theory-building research objectives are important to legal scholarship as they allow grasping the law as a system, abstracting from particularities to generalities.[40] In this respect, a theory-building research objective goes beyond describing, comparing and classifying legal constructs. By looking beyond details and particularities, legal scholars try to uncover the essentials of legal constructs, including their effects and consequences. The result is a theoretical framework that covers the practical application of law, with all its details and specifics.

Despite the importance of theory-building, legal scholars tend to be rather reticent about it. Most legal scholars have the feeling that "theory-building is something mysterious and only reserved to a few".[41] VAN GESTEL urges legal scholars to get rid of this thought, but at the same time criticizes the uncertainty about theory-building in legal scholarship. Not only its scope and meaning, but also its merits within legal scholarship remain rather unclear.[42]

---

36 M. VAN HOECKE, "Aard en methode van de rechtsdogmatiek", *R & R* 1984, 199. See also: W. TWINING, *Law in context,* Oxford, Clarendon Press, 1997, 135.

37 This definition is a combination of VAN HOECKE and VAN GESTEL: M. VAN HOECKE, "Legal Doctrine: Which Method(s) for What Kind of Discipline", in M. VAN HOECKE (ed.), *Methodologies of Legal Research*, Oxford, Hart Publishing, 2011, 15; R.A.J. VAN GESTEL, Preadvies "Kwaliteit van juridische publicaties. Over ranking, peer review, sciëntometrics en vertrouwen in alternatieve evaluatiemethoden" in HANDELINGEN NEDERLANDSE JURISTEN-VERENIGING, *Kwaliteit als keuze in rechtspraak, wetgeving en rechtswetenschap,* Deventer, Kluwer, 2015, 338–339.

38 Example from: M. BARENDRECHT, J. VRANKEN, I. GIESEN, M.J. BORGERS, W. VAN DER BURG, H.E.B. TIJSSEN, G.C.G.J. VAN ROERMUND and W.H. VAN BOOM, "Methoden van rechtswetenschap: komen we verder?", *NJB* 2004, 1425.

39 J.M. BARENDRECHT, "Rechtswetenschap: stoffig of inventief?", *NJB* 1996, 714.

40 P. SCHOLTEN, "Algemeen Deel" in *Asser's Handleiding tot de beoefening van het Nederlandsch Burgerlijk Recht,* Zwolle, W.E.J. Tjeenk Willink, 1954, 75. See also: W. TWINING, *Law in context,* Oxford, Clarendon Press, 1997, 134.

41 Translation of: "theorievorming een geheimzinnig iets is dat maar voor weinigen is weggelegd."R.A.J VAN GESTEL, Preadvies "Kwaliteit van juridische publicaties. Over ranking, peer review, sciëntometrics en vertrouwen in alternatieve evaluatiemethoden" in HANDELINGEN NEDERLANDSE JURISTEN-VERENIGING, *Kwaliteit als keuze in rechtspraak, wetgeving en rechtswetenschap,* Deventer, Kluwer, 2015, 336.

42 R.A.J VAN GESTEL, Preadvies "Kwaliteit van juridische publicaties. Over ranking, peer review, sciëntometrics en vertrouwen in alternatieve evaluatiemethoden" in HANDELINGEN NEDERLANDSE JURISTEN-VERENIGING, *Kwaliteit als keuze in*

2.5 EXPLANATORY RESEARCH OBJECTIVE

An explanatory research objective aims to clarify why a particular legal construct exists.[43] It is not about describing what something is, but about explaining "why something is as it is."[44] The emphasis lies on the causes, motives, background and roots of law.[45]

Explanatory research objectives are important as they contribute to a better understanding of the existence, content and subsequent modifications of legal rules. However, VAN HOECKE points out that searching for an explanation of legal rules is not really popular in legal scholarship.[46] This is confirmed by an empirical study at Dutch law faculties showing that their academic staff is not really familiar with *why* questions.[47] Moreover, the meta-study of our PhD project also showed that explanatory research objectives are often overshadowed by the other objectives of a research.[48]

It is unfortunate that explanatory research objectives stay in the background too often. Especially because of their importance for formulating future recommendations. VRANKEN is of the opinion that too often legal scholars look for solutions without prior investigating the actual problem: *what* is the problem, *to whom* is it a problem, *why* is it a problem?[49] Without understanding the underlying problem, a recommendation can never offer a suitable solution: "it is like prescribing a medicine, without a diagnosis of the complaint."[50]

---

rechtspraak, wetgeving en rechtswetenschap, Deventer, Kluwer, 2015, 339. See also: J.B.M. VRANKEN, "Een nieuw rechtsrealisme in het privaatrecht", *WPNR* 2011, 1121.

43 M. VAN HOECKE, "Hoe wetenschappelijk is de rechtswetenschap?", *TPR* 2009, 649; G.A.F.M. VAN SCHAAIJK, *Praktijkgericht juridisch onderzoek*, The Hague, Boom Juridische uitgevers, 2011, 72.

44 H.A. OOST, *De kwaliteit van probleemstellingen in dissertaties*, Utrecht, Elinkwijk, 1999, 58.

45 I. CURRY-SUMNER, F. KIRSTEN, T. VAN DER LINDEN-SMITH and J. TIGCHELAAR, *Onderzoeksvaardigheden*, Nijmegen, Ars Aequi Libri, 2010, 18; R.A.J. VAN GESTEL and J.B.M. VRANKEN, "Rechtswetenschappelijke artikelen", *NJB* 2007, 1454.

46 M. VAN HOECKE, "Hoe wetenschappelijk is de rechtswetenschap?", *TPR* 2009, 650.

47 W. VAN BOOM and R. VAN GESTEL, "Rechtswetenschappelijk onderzoek. Een samenvatting van de uitkomsten van een landelijke enquête", *NJB* 2015, (full version available online), 11 and 34.

48 L. KESTEMONT, *Naar een rechtswetenschappelijke methodeleer. Een expliciet methodologisch kader voor rechtswetenschappelijk onderzoek in het socialezekerheidsrecht*, Bruges, die Keure (reeks Begasoz/ Abetrass), 2017, 201.

49 J.B.M. VRANKEN, "Algemeen Deel. Een synthese" in *Mr. C. Assers Handleiding tot de beoefening van het Nederlands Burgerlijk Recht*, Deventer, Kluwer, 2014, 52.

50 Translation of: "het lijkt op het voorschrijven van een medicijn zonder diagnose van de ziekte."J.B.M. VRANKEN, "Algemeen Deel. Een synthese" in *Mr. C. Assers Handleiding tot de beoefening van het Nederlands Burgerlijk Recht*, Deventer, Kluwer, 2014, 53.

2.6 EVALUATIVE RESEARCH OBJECTIVE

An evaluative research objective aims to assess/evaluate a legal construct in view of a 'norm'.[51] Many authors believe that evaluating the law is a *duty* of legal scholarship.[52] As legal scholars are bound by current law to a lesser degree than legislators or judges, they are in the best position to distance themselves for a critical assessment.

An evaluative research objective can assess whether a legal construct attains its goals or solves a specific problem, whether it is in compliance with a general principle of law, whether it violates a supranational legal norm, etc. As legal scholars can put forward different 'norms', evaluations in legal scholarship can be quite diverse.[53]

The results of an evaluative research objective will play an important role when legal scholars aim to formulate recommendations at the end of their research.[54] However, they remain two distinct objectives: an evaluative research objective results in the evaluation of a legal construct, whereas a recommendatory research objective goes a step further and recommends how the legal construct *should* be. Consequently, both objectives correspond to a different phase of the research and require their own methodological approach.

2.7 RECOMMENDATORY RESEARCH OBJECTIVE

Finally, as discussed above, recommendatory research objectives aim to determine how the law *should* be. This type of research objective reflects the "solution-oriented attitude" of legal scholars "to carry out improvements or changes to arrive at a fairer functioning of the law or a more efficient and effective functioning."[55] Not

---

51 H. TIJSSEN, *De juridische dissertatie onder de loep*, The Hague, Boom Juridische uitgevers, 2009, 58.

52 A.R. BLOEMBERGEN, "Iets over object en methode van wetenschap en rechtspraak in het privaatrecht" in O.W.M. KAMSTRA, F.B.M. KUNNEMAN and C.W. MARIS (eds.), *Nederlandse rechtswetenschap. Tussen distantie en betrokkenheid: paradigma's in de twingtigste eeuw*, Zwolle, W.E.J. Tjeenk Willink, 1988, 76; M. VERHORST, "De rechtswetenschappelijke gemeenschap" in O.W.M. KAMSTRA, F.B.M. KUNNEMAN and C.W. MARIS (eds.), *Nederlandse rechtswetenschap. Tussen distantie en betrokkenheid: paradigma's in de twintigste eeuw*, Zwolle, W.E.J. Tjeenk Willink, 1988, 355.

53 L. KESTEMONT, *Naar een rechtswetenschappelijke methodeleer. Een expliciet methodologisch kader voor rechtswetenschappelijk onderzoek in het socialezekerheidsrecht*, Bruges, die Keure (reeks Begasoz/ Abetrass), 2017, 203.

54 A.R. MACKOR, "Legal Doctrine As a Non-Normative Discipline", *Recht en Methode* 2012 (1), 24; H. TIJSSEN, *De juridische dissertatie onder de loep*, The Hague, Boom Juridische uitgevers, 2009, 59.

55 Translation of: "Opvallend is dat de onderzoeker vrijwel altijd onderzoek doet vanuit een oplossingsgerichte attitude; zijn doel is primair om verbeteringen of veranderingen te willen doorvoeren met het oog op een rechtvaardiger functioneren van het recht of gericht op het streven naar een effectieve en efficiënte werking ervan." H. TIJSSEN, *De juridische dissertatie onder de loep*, The Hague, Boom Juridische uitgevers, 2009, 165. See also HUTCHINSON

only academic literature acknowledges that the formulation of recommendations is typical for legal scholarship[56], it is also confirmed by empirical research. For example, a research at Dutch law faculties has shown that their academic staff characterize their publications mainly as proposals for improvement of existing law.[57] In addition, the meta-study of our PhD project indicated that the formulation of recommendations was the main research objective in more than 2/3 of the studied PhDs.[58] Despite the popularity of recommendatory research objectives, VRANKEN questions legal scholars' urge to formulate recommendations. He notices that "in legal research it is almost self-evident that current law is not proper. Even before shortcomings – and if so which ones – are ascertained, measures for improvement are already been recommended."[59]

To conclude, a recommendatory research objective results in a proposal to enact, complete, modify or abolish law. The effects of the recommendation should allow for existing problems, such as inconsistencies or lacunas, to be solved or at least ameliorated.[60]

---

about 'reform perspective': T. HUTCHINSON, "Doctrinal research" in D. WATKINS and M. BURTON (eds.), *Research Methods in Law*, London, Routledge, 23; J.B.M. VRANKEN, "Algemeen Deel. Een synthese" in *Mr. C. Assers Handleiding tot de beoefening van het Nederlands Burgerlijk Recht*, Deventer, Kluwer, 2014, 10.

56 F. KUNNEMAN, *Rechtswetenschap*, Nijmegen, Ars Aequi Libri, 1991, 8; E.L. RUBIN, "Law and the Methodology of Law", *Wis.L.Rev.* 1997, 523; E.M.H. HIRSCH BALLIN, "Object en methode van de wetenschap van het staatsrecht en het bestuursrecht" in O.W.M. KAMSTRA, F.B.M. KUNNEMAN and C.W. MARIS (eds.), *Nederlandse rechtswetenschap. Tussen distantie en betrokkenheid: paradigma's in de twingtigste eeuw*, Zwolle, W.E.J. Tjeenk Willink, 1988, 86; E.L. RUBIN, "The Practice and Discourse of Legal Scholarship", *Mich.L.Rev.* 1987–88, 1847; C. STOLKER, "Een discipline in transitie, *ReM* 2011, afl. 1, 23; J. VRANKEN, "Exiciting Times for Legal Scholarship", *ReM* 2012, afl. 2, 48; M. VAN HOECKE, "Aard en methode van de rechtsdogmatiek", *R & R* 1984, 188; R.A.J. VAN GESTEL and J.B.M. VRANKEN, "Rechtswetenschappelijke artikelen", *NJB* 2007, 1455; D.W. VICK, "Interdisciplinarity and the Discipline of Law", *Brit.J.Law & Soc.* 2004,179; J.B.M. VRANKEN, "Nieuwe richtingen in de rechtswetenschap, *WPNR* 2010, 322; P. WESTERMAN and M. WISSINK, "Rechtsgeleerdheid als rechtswetenschap", *NJB* 2008, 505; M. VAN HOECKE, "Legal Doctrine: Which Method(s) for What Kind of Discipline?" in M. VAN HOECKE (ed.), *Methodologies of Legal Research*, Oxford, Hart Publishing, 2011, 10; J. HAGE, "The Method of a Truly Normative Legal Science" in M. VAN HOECKE (ed.), *Methodologies of Legal Research*, Oxford, Hart Publishing, 2011, 29.

57 W. VAN BOOM and R. VAN GESTEL, "Rechtswetenschappelijk onderzoek. Een samenvatting van de uitkomsten van een landelijke enquête", *NJB 2015* (full version available online), 11.

58 L. KESTEMONT, *Naar een rechtswetenschappelijke methodeleer. Een expliciet methodologisch kader voor rechtswetenschappelijk onderzoek in het socialezekerheidsrecht*, Bruges, die Keure (reeks Begasoz/ Abetrass), 2017, 112.

59 Translation of: "het bijna vanzelfsprekende uitgangspunt bij juridisch onderzoek is dat het huidige recht niet goed is. Nog voordat is vastgesteld of er wel tekortkomingen zijn en zo ja welke, komen al verbetermaatregelen in zicht." J.B.M. VRANKEN, "Als een arrest niet bevalt, laten wij het gewoon weg" in H. NIEUWENHUIS (ed.), *Ex Libris*, Deventer, Kluwer, 2009, 86.

60 F. KUNNEMAN, *Rechtswetenschap*, Nijmegen, Ars Aequi Libri, 1991, 9; H. TIJSSEN, *De juridische dissertatie onder de loep*, The Hague, Boom Juridische uitgevers, 2009, 59, 74 en 165.

3 RESEARCH OBJECTIVES AND THEIR METHODOLOGICAL FEATURES

In part 3 of this handbook we continue by discussing the methodological features of each type of research objective.

3.1 METHODOLOGICAL FEATURES OF A DESCRIPTIVE RESEARCH OBJECTIVE

A descriptive research objective will systematically analyze legal constructs in all their components in order to present them in an accurate, significant and orderly manner. In this section we shed light on the angle and the structure of a description, we clarify nine different types of interpretation and we explain that in the process of interpreting legal rules sometimes normative choices have to be made.

3.1.1 DESCRIPTION ANGLE

As law is mainly laid down in legal texts; the interpretation of these texts is important when describing the law. It involves "the attribution of a meaning to a document, or to a set of documents, which is (are) regarded as expressing a legal norm."[1] Every interpretation departs from a particular perspective: the background of a regulation, the structure of a legal system, the purpose of legal rule, etc.[2] Also the sources used for interpretation are of importance. After all, an interpretation on the basis of current case law can be different from an interpretation on the basis of parliamentary preparatory works. Legal scholars therefore always have to clarify which sources were used to interpret a legal construct.[3]

1 P. NERHOT, "Interpretation in Legal Science" in P. NERHOT (ed.), *Law, Interpretation and Reality*, Dordrecht, Kluwer, 1990, 197.

2 F. KUNNEMAN, *Rechtswetenschap*, Nijmegen, Ars Aequi Libri, 1991, 4; P. SCHOLTEN, "De structuur der rechtswetenschap" in *Verzamelde Geschriften van wijlen Prof. Mr. Paul Scholten*, Zwolle, Tjeenk Willink, 1949, 457; C.W. MARIS, "Distantie en betrokkenheid in de rechtswetenschap" in O.W.M. KAMSTRA, F.B.M. KUNNEMAN and C.W. MARIS (eds.), *Nederlandse rechtswetenschap. Tussen distantie en betrokkenheid: paradigma's in de twingtigste eeuw*, Zwolle, W.E.J. Tjeenk Willink, 1988, 6.

3 N. HOEKX, K. VANHOVE and A. VERBEKE, "Yes we care! Bedenkingen over de (methode der) rechtswetenschap", *RW* 2008–09, 1787.

A descriptive research objective is often a preliminary step, to the benefit of the other objectives of the research, such as classifications, comparisons, evaluations etc. Those other research goals will influence the interpretation of legal rules and judgments.[4] After all, they determine to a large extent the description angle: is an old regulation being described in order to compare it with its renewed counterpart, or in order to analyze whether its scope of application could also cover a new social phenomenon? Moreover, the extent to which a researcher takes into account non-applicable law, such as old legislation or rejected bills, also depends on the description's purpose for the other research goals.

3.1.2 DESCRIPTION STRUCTURE

Legal scholars can divide their description into different parts or can structure it according to themes. For example, a description of legislation on medical check-ups in case of invalidity can be divided/structured according to the type of invalidity: industrial accidents, occupational diseases, pregnancy, etc.[5] Using a fixed description structure can be useful when describing different regulations, as it allows to describe distinct regulations in a similar way, thereby avoiding repetitions.

Legal scholars can opt for a description structure that corresponds to the existing legal framework. For example, a comparative legal research on social risks can decide to describe national social insurance schemes according to the subdivision in EU Regulation 883/2004 on the coordination of social security systems: a) sickness benefits, b) maternity and equivalent paternity benefits, c) invalidity benefits, d) old-age benefits, e) survivors' benefits, f) benefits in respect of accidents at work and occupational diseases, g) death grants, h) unemployment benefits, i) pre-retirement benefits and j) family benefits.[6]

Legal researchers can also propose their own description structure. This might be interesting when a research is focusing on a specific set of provisions in different regulations or on similar modalities in different contracts. In the latter case, a researcher can first classify the different modalities and types of contracts and subsequently use this classification to determine the description's structure.

---

4 J.B.M. VRANKEN, "Algemeen Deel. Een synthese" in *Mr. C. Assers Handleiding tot de beoefening van het Nederlands Burgerlijk Recht*, Deventer, Kluwer, 2014, 131.

5 Example from the meta-study of 45 PhDs on social security law: K. SCHUTYSER, K., *De geneeskundige controle in de sociale zekerheid*, 1973, PhD KU Leuven.

6 Example from the meta-study of 45 PhDs on social security law: P. SCHOUKENS, *De sociale zekerheid van de zelfstandige en het Europese Gemeenschapsrecht: de impact van het vrije verkeer van zelfstandigen*, 1999, PhD KU Leuven.

3.1.3 DIFFERENT TYPES OF INTERPRETATION

Legal scholars can opt for different types of interpretation.[7] We distinguish nine types: grammatical interpretation, technical interpretation, systematic interpretation, legal-historical interpretation, teleological interpretation, interpretation on the basis of jurisprudence, interpretation on the basis of legal doctrine, interpretation on the basis of non-binding legal sources, and sociological interpretation.[8]

There is no hierarchy between these different types of interpretations.[9] The choice for a specific type of interpretation depends on the researcher and the description angle. As every type of interpretation departs from a specific point of view (grammar, legal history, legislator's objectives, etc.) they all have their shortcomings. It is therefore advisable to combine different interpretations.[10]

In the following the different types of interpretations are discussed separately. However, some interpretations are heavily intertwined and sometimes even

---

7 J.B.M. VRANKEN, "Algemeen Deel. Een synthese" in *Mr. C. Assers Handleiding tot de beoefening van het Nederlands Burgerlijk Recht*, Deventer, Kluwer, 2014, 135; D.N. MACCORMICK and R.S. SUMMERS (eds.), *Interpreting Statutes*, Aldershot, Dartmouth, 1991, 567 p.; P. SCHOLTEN, "Algemeen Deel" in *Asser's Handleiding tot de beoefening van het Nederlandsch Burgerlijk Recht*, Zwolle, W.E.J. Tjeenk Willink, 1954, 4; G.A.F.M. VAN SCHAAIJK, *Praktijkgericht juridisch onderzoek*, The Hague, Boom Juridische uitgevers, 2011, 104–105.

8 See: G. DE GEEST, "Hoe maken we van de rechtswetenschap een volwaardige wetenschap?", *NJB* 2004, 59 and 61; M. BARENDRECHT, J. VRANKEN, I. GIESEN, M.J. BORGERS, W. VAN DER BURG, H.E.B. TIJSSEN, G.C.G.J. VAN ROERMUND and W.H. VAN BOOM, "Methoden van rechtswetenschap: komen we verder?", *NJB* 2004, 1424; M. VAN HOECKE, "Aard en methode van de rechtsdogmatiek", *R & R* 1984, 202; E.L. RUBIN, "Law and the Methodology of Law", *Wis.L.Rev.* 1997, 528. For more information on types of interpretation see: F.T. GROENEWEGEN, *Wetsinterpretatie en rechtsvorming*, The Hague, Boom Juridische uitgevers, 2006, 79–187; P. DELNOY, *Eléments de méthodologie juridique*, Brussels, Larcier, 2008, 155–180; P.G. KORREL and O.W.M. KAMSTRA, *Sociaal wetenschappelijke & juridische methodologie*, Amsterdam, Melkman, 1991, 121; R. KRANENBURG, *De grondslagen der rechtswetenschap*, Haarlem, Tjeenk Willink, 1952, 32.

9 M. VAN HOECKE, "Aard en methode van de rechtsdogmatiek", *R & R* 1984, 202; F.T. GROENEWEGEN, *Wetsinterpretatie en rechtsvorming*, The Hague, Boom Juridische uitgevers, 2006, 185–190; G.E. LANGEMEIJER, "Recht en Rechtsbeschouwing in de tweede helft van de Twintigste Eeuw" in J.M. POLAK, *Vooruitzichten van de* Rechtswetenschap, Deventer, Kluwer, 1964, 25; P. SCHOLTEN, "Algemeen Deel" in *Asser's Handleiding tot de beoefening van het Nederlandsch Burgerlijk Recht*, Zwolle, W.E.J. Tjeenk Willink, 1954, 48; P.W. KAMPHUISEN, *Beschouwingen over rechtswetenschap*, Nijmegen, Dekker & Van De Vegt, 1938, 61; P. VAN BEMMELEN, *Regtsgeleerde opstellen*, I, Leiden, E.J. Brill, 1891, 7; J.B.M. VRANKEN, "Algemeen Deel. Een synthese" in *Mr. C. Assers Handleiding tot de beoefening van het Nederlands Burgerlijk Recht*, Deventer, Kluwer, 2014, 131; E. EGGERMONT, M. GEUENS, F. GOWIE and E. TIMBERMONT, *Het juridisch verwerkingsproces*, Bruges, die Keure, 2014, 117.

10 VAN HOECKE demonstrates in his PhD the necessity of such combination: M. VAN HOECKE, *De interpretatievrijheid van de rechter*, Antwerp, Kluwer, 1979, 72–330. See also: F.T. GROENEWEGEN, *Wetsinterpretatie en rechtsvorming*, The Hague, Boom Juridische uitgevers, 2006, 88–89; J.J.H. BRUGGINK, *Wat zegt Scholten over recht*, Zwolle, W.E.J. Tjeenk Willink, 1983, 167.

convert to each other.[11] Moreover, interpretation is also a matter of different dimensions. For instance, an interpretation on the basis of jurisprudence looks at the opinions of judges, who in order to come to their opinions had to interpret legal sources themselves.

3.1.3.1 Grammatical interpretation

A grammatical interpretation interprets a legal provision on the basis of its grammar, syntax and choice of words. The first step consists of isolating the essential words (e.g. substantives, adjectives, verbs, etc.) and clarifying their meaning.[12] A grammatical interpretation always uses the literal meaning of words, or their meaning in common parlance.[13] For this legal scholars can rely on dictionaries.[14] However, it is important to be aware that dictionaries very often provide several definitions for the same word, all depending on the context.[15]

In a second step, the researcher ends the isolation and concentrates on how different parts of a sentence relate to each other.[16] For this purpose, it is important to parse the sentence[17]: what is the subject, what is the form of the

---

11 M. VAN HOECKE, *De interpretatievrijheid van de rechter*, Antwerp, Kluwer, 1979, 72–330. See also: J.M. POLAK, *Theorie en practijk der rechtsvinding*, Zwolle, W.E.J. Tjeenk Willink, 1953, 37.

12 LARENZ refers to the "*Wortsinn*": K. LARENZ, *Methodenlehre der Rechtswissenschaft*, Berlin, Springer, 1983, 305; E.M. MEIJERS, *Dogmatische rechtswetenschap*, 's-Gravenhage, Belinfante, 1903, 139.

13 F.T. GROENEWEGEN, *Wetsinterpretatie en rechtsvorming*, The Hague, Boom Juridische uitgevers, 2006, 79; P. DELNOY, *Eléments de méthodologie juridique*, Brussels, Larcier, 2008, 155; H.F. JOLOWICZ, *Lectures on Jurisprudence*, London, Athlone Press, 1963, 281; H. FRANKEN, *Encyclopedie van de rechtswetenschap*, Deventer, Gouda Quint, 2001, 195; J.J.H. BRUGGINK, *Wat zegt Scholten over recht*, Zwolle, W.E.J. Tjeenk Willink, 1983, 155; A. PECZENIK, *On Law and Reason*, Dordrecht, Kluwer, 1989, 381; G.A.F.M. VAN SCHAAIJK, *Praktijkgericht juridisch onderzoek*, The Hague, Boom Juridische uitgevers, 2011, 106; P.W. KAMPHUISEN, *Beschouwingen over rechtswetenschap*, Nijmegen, Dekker & Van De Vegt, 1938, 59; E.M. MEIJERS, *Dogmatische rechtswetenschap*, 's-Gravenhage, Belinfante, 1903, 138; J. BELL and G. ENGLE, *Cross: Statutory Interpretation*, London, Butterworths, 1995, 109; E. EGGERMONT, M. GEUENS, F. GOWIE and E. TIMBERMONT, *Het juridisch verwerkingsproces*, Bruges, die Keure, 2014, 120.

14 F.T. GROENEWEGEN, *Wetsinterpretatie en rechtsvorming*, The Hague, Boom Juridische uitgevers, 2006, 81; M. VAN HOECKE, *De interpretatievrijheid van de rechter*, Antwerp, Kluwer, 1979, 111.

15 F.T. GROENEWEGEN, *Wetsinterpretatie en rechtsvorming*, The Hague, Boom Juridische uitgevers, 2006, 813.

16 E.M. MEIJERS, *Dogmatische rechtswetenschap*, 's-Gravenhage, Belinfante, 1903, 139; P. SCHOLTEN, "Algemeen Deel" in *Asser's Handleiding tot de beoefening van het Nederlandsch Burgerlijk Recht*, Zwolle, W.E.J. Tjeenk Willink, 1954, 50; M. VAN HOECKE, *De interpretatievrijheid van de rechter*, Antwerp, Kluwer, 1979, 140.

17 F.T. GROENEWEGEN, *Wetsinterpretatie en rechtsvorming*, The Hague, Boom Juridische uitgevers, 2006, 84.

verb, etc.[18] Also the place of conjunctions and punctuation marks can have implications for the meaning of a part of, or even for the whole sentence.[19]

A grammatical interpretation has different flaws. First of all, it is possible that the legislator's actual intention is insufficiently reflected in the grammar, syntax or choice of words of a legal provision. A grammatical interpretation is therefore useless when a legal text contains vague or ambiguous words.[20]

Second, writers of legal texts can make a wrong choice of words or grammatical mistakes.[21] It is also possible that different meanings of words were insufficiently considered.[22] This will of course hinder a grammatical interpretation.

Third, an interpretation based on grammar, syntax and *natural language* keeps the scope of legal texts rather limited.[23] An extension of their scope because of changes in other legislation, developments in society, new case law or legal doctrines is not considered when pursuing a grammatical interpretation.

Finally, a grammatical interpretation has to be used carefully in case of international legal texts that were translated into different languages. The same is true for national legislation drafted in different national languages.[24] After all, a linguistic nuance in one language does not always have an equivalent in another language, or the same concept can have a different meaning in other languages.[25] Moreover, it even occurs that translations of legal texts use words with a slightly different meaning. An example is Article 6 of the European Convention on Human Rights: "the *determination* of his civil rights and obligations" versus the French version "des *contestations* sur ses droits et obligations de caractère civil."

3.1.3.2 Technical interpretation

Although legal rules are written down in standard language, law as a discipline also has its own (technical) jargon. Most of the time, however, the meaning of legal jargon is self-evident for legal scholars:

---

18 P. GOODRICH, *Reading the Law. A Critical Introduction to Legal Method and Techniques*, Oxford, Basil Blackwell, 1986, 111.

19 P. DELNOY, *Eléments de méthodologie juridique*, Brussels, Larcier, 2008, 155.

20 F.T. GROENEWEGEN, *Wetsinterpretatie en rechtsvorming*, The Hague, Boom Juridische uitgevers, 2006, 87.

21 P. SCHOLTEN, "Algemeen Deel" in *Asser's Handleiding tot de beoefening van het Nederlandsch Burgerlijk Recht*, Zwolle, W.E.J. Tjeenk Willink, 1954, 53–54.

22 M. VAN HOECKE, *De interpretatievrijheid van de rechter*, Antwerp, Kluwer, 1979, 92.

23 A. PECZENIK, "Scientia Juris. Legal Doctrine as knowledge of Law and as a Source of Law" in E. PATTARO (ed.), *A Treatise of Legal Philosophy and General Jurisprudence*, Dordrecht, Springer, 2005, 20.

24 M. VAN HOECKE, *De interpretatievrijheid van de rechter*, Antwerp, Kluwer, 1979, 193.

25 J. BELL and G. ENGLE, *Cross: Statutory Interpretation*, London, Butterworths, 1995, 109; P. DELNOY, *Eléments de méthodologie juridique*, Brussels, Larcier, 2008, 163.

"if the context is a technical one, a word which has both an ordinary and a technical meaning must be interpreted in its technical sense, and this is particularly true in the case of words having a technical legal sense. Nobody imagines, for example, that the Prescription Act deals with the medicines that doctors prescribe for their patients."[26]

Regardless of this self-evidence, it nevertheless concerns an interpretation. More specifically, an interpretation from a technical-legal point of view.[27] Sometimes legal scholars will consider the meaning of legal jargon more consciously: for example, when a legal concept has a very specific meaning within one particular branch of law, or when the exact scope of the concept is unclear/under discussion.

A technical interpretation can also relate to technical non-legal jargon that is common to particular professions or sectors.[28] Such jargon will often be found in legislation regulating technical matters, such as safety rules for machinery or prohibited substances in drugs.

3.1.3.3 Systematic interpretation

A systematic interpretation interprets legal provisions on the basis of their place within the broader legal system and in view of other legal provisions.[29] A systematic interpretation will try to avoid conflicts between different legal rules[30]:

"From the unity follows that each legal provision has to be clarified in connection to the others. Not only are words of one provision frequently made comprehensible

---

26 H.F. JOLOWICZ, *Lectures on Jurisprudence,* London, Athlone Press, 1963, 281. See also: H. FRANKEN, *Encyclopedie van de rechtswetenschap,* Deventer, Gouda Quint, 2001, 282.

27 P. SCHOLTEN, "Algemeen Deel" in *Asser's Handleiding tot de beoefening van het Nederlandsch Burgerlijk Recht,* Zwolle, W.E.J. Tjeenk Willink, 1954, 51; J.J.H. BRUGGINK, *Wat zegt Scholten over recht,* Zwolle, W.E.J. Tjeenk Willink, 1983, 155–156; See also: A. PECZENIK, *On Law and Reason,* Dordrecht, Kluwer, 1989, 383.

28 SUMMERS and TARUFFO discuss 'legal technical words' and 'non-legal technical words.' See R.S. SUMMERS and M. TARUFFO, "Interpretation and Comparative Analysis" in D.N. MACCORMICK and R.S. SUMMERS (eds.), *Interpreting Statutes,* Aldershot, Dartmouth, 1991, 464; M. VAN HOECKE, *De interpretatievrijheid van de rechter,* Antwerp, Kluwer, 1979, 109.

29 P. DELNOY, *Eléments de méthodologie juridique,* Brussels, Larcier, 2008, 165; A. PECZENIK, "Scientia Juris. Legal Doctrine as knowledge of Law and as a Source of Law" in E. PATTARO (ed.), *A Treatise of Legal Philosopy and General Jurisprudence,* Dordrecht, Springer, 2005, 19; F.T. GROENEWEGEN, *Wetsinterpretatie en rechtsvorming,* The Hague, Boom Juridische uitgevers, 2006, 125; H. FRANKEN, *Encyclopedie van de rechtswetenschap,* Deventer, Gouda Quint, 2001, 196; R. KRANENBURG, *De grondslagen der rechtswetenschap,* Haarlem, Tjeenk Willink, 1952, 32; J.J.H. BRUGGINK, *Wat zegt Scholten over recht,* Zwolle, W.E.J. Tjeenk Willink, 1983, 160; M. VAN HOECKE, *De interpretatievrijheid van de rechter,* Antwerp, Kluwer, 1979, 146.

30 H. FRANKEN, *Encyclopedie van de rechtswetenschap,* Deventer, Gouda Quint, 2001, 196. See also: E. STEINER, *French Legal Method,* Oxford, Oxford University Press, 2002, 66.

by the words of another provision, we also try to understand different provisions in such a way that they form a contiguous unity. One thing is always considered as an implementation, completion or deviation of something else."[31]

In a first step, the legal researcher will situate the provision within the structure of the overall regulation: under which chapter, section, title and/or paragraph is the provision situated[32], is the provision referring to other provisions within the same regulation and/or vice versa?[33] Both preambles and definitions at the beginning of a regulation can provide essential information.[34]

In a second step, the legal scholar situates the provision within the structure of the overall legal system: does the provision refer to (provisions in) other regulations and/or vice versa[35], what is the place of the regulation – containing the provision – in a specific Code or area of law?[36] The hierarchy of norms will play an important role: a higher legal norm can determine the meaning of a lower legal norm, not the other way around.[37] European and international legal norms can therefore be extremely relevant in the case of a systematic interpretation.[38] Also customary law and legal principles have to be taken into account.[39] After all, a legal provision can be a specific application of a legal principle.[40]

---

31 Translation of: "Uit die eenheid volgt ook, dat iedere wetsbepaling steeds in verband met andere moet worden uitgelegd. Niet alleen dat de woorden van het ene artikel dikwijls eerst verstaanbaar worden door die van het andere, we trachten ook de verschillende wetsvoorschriften zoo te begrijpen, dat zij een aansluitend geheel vormen. Het eene wordt gezien als uitwerking, aanvulling of afwijking van het andere." P. SCHOLTEN, "Algemeen Deel" in *Asser's Handleiding tot de beoefening van het Nederlandsch Burgerlijk Recht*, Zwolle, W.E.J. Tjeenk Willink, 1954, 60.

32 M. VAN HOECKE, *De interpretatievrijheid van de rechter*, Antwerp, Kluwer, 1979, 147; J.M. POLAK, *Theorie en practijk der rechtsvinding*, Zwolle, W.E.J. Tjeenk Willink, 1953, 29.

33 P. DELNOY, *Eléments de méthodologie juridique*, Brussels, Larcier, 2008, 166–167; A. PECZENIK, "Scientia Juris. Legal Doctrine as knowledge of Law and as a Source of Law" in E. PATTARO (ed.), *A Treatise of Legal Philosopy and General Jurisprudence*, Dordrecht, Springer, 2005, 19; F.T. GROENEWEGEN, *Wetsinterpretatie en rechtsvorming*, The Hague, Boom Juridische uitgevers, 2006, 142; N. MACCORMICK, *Rhetoric and the Rule of* Law, Oxford, Oxford University Press, 2005, 128.

34 F.T. GROENEWEGEN, *Wetsinterpretatie en rechtsvorming*, The Hague, Boom Juridische uitgevers, 2006, 92 en 143; P. GOODRICH, *Reading the Law. A Critical Introduction to Legal Method and Techniques*, Oxford, Basil Blackwell, 1986, 113.

35 N. MACCORMICK, *Rhetoric and the Rule of* Law, Oxford, Oxford University Press, 2005, 128.

36 G.A.F.M. VAN SCHAAIJK, *Praktijkgericht juridisch onderzoek*, The Hague, Boom Juridische uitgevers, 2011, 107; J. BELL and G. ENGLE, *Cross: Statutory Interpretation*, London, Butterworths, 1995, 111 (referring to interpretations of EU-provisions).

37 M. VAN HOECKE, *De interpretatievrijheid van de rechter*, Antwerp, Kluwer, 1979, 150–151.

38 R. VAN GESTEL and H.-W. MICKLITZ, "Revitalising Doctrinal Legal Research in Europe: What About Methodology?" in U. NEERGAARD, R. NIELSEN and L. ROSEBERRY (eds.), *European Legal Method – Paradoxes and Revitalisation*, Kopenhagen, DJØF Publishing, 2011, 67.

39 F.T. GROENEWEGEN, *Wetsinterpretatie en rechtsvorming*, The Hague, Boom Juridische uitgevers, 2006, 154; M. VAN HOECKE, *De interpretatievrijheid van de rechter*, Antwerp, Kluwer, 1979, 146.

40 See also: D.N. MACCORMICK en R.S. SUMMERS, "Interpretation and Justification" in D.N. MACCORMICK and R.S. SUMMERS (eds.), *Interpreting Statutes*, Aldershot, Dartmouth, 1991, 514.

Preparatory works can be a useful source of information. They often contain an indication of the place of a provision within the legal system.[41] Also regulations – and their preparatory works – that are not yet implemented could be interesting to look at when they intend to change existing rules and/or the structure of a legal system. Legal scholars may decide to anticipate this change in a systematic interpretation.[42] However, they should check the progress of the legislative procedure: a bill at the end of its procedure is more influential than a bill only recently introduced in Parliament.[43]

Some caution needs to be exercised when using a systematic interpretation. First of all, titles of legislation, chapters or sections can suffer from incompleteness, inaccuracy or even mistakes.[44] Moreover, titles of legislative acts, chapters and sections do not have any normative means.[45] DELNOY clarified this by referring to (ex) Article 373 of the Belgian Code of Criminal Procedure.[46] This article stated that an appeal in cassation had a suspensive effect for the execution of a judgment. This legal provision came under the title "Cases dealt with by a jury". A purely systematic interpretation would conclude that the suspensive effect of an appeal in cassation only applies to Assize Court cases. However, the same rule was in fact applicable to cases before criminal courts. In sum, the mere fact that the provision was situated under the chapter on jury trials was in itself not enough to conclude that it only applied to those trials.

Second, the same legal concept can appear in different regulations. It is therefore tempting to apply a similar conceptual interpretation for all regulations. However, because of the differences between areas of law (private law, economic law, social law, etc.) and differences in legislative contexts, these kinds of uniform/universal definitions are far from obvious.[47] An example would be the concept of 'wage'. It appears both in the Belgian Act on the protection of

---

41 F.T. GROENEWEGEN, *Wetsinterpretatie en rechtsvorming*, The Hague, Boom Juridische uitgevers, 2006, 121–122 en 142.

42 F.T. GROENEWEGEN, *Wetsinterpretatie en rechtsvorming*, The Hague, Boom Juridische uitgevers, 2006, 127; H. FRANKEN, *Encyclopedie van de rechtswetenschap*, Deventer, Gouda Quint, 2001, 197; J.B.M. VRANKEN, "Algemeen Deel" in *Asser's Handleiding tot de beoefening van het Nederlands Burgerlijk Recht*, Zwolle, W.E.J. Tjeenk Willink, 1995, 102 ff.; M. VAN HOECKE, *De interpretatievrijheid van de rechter*, Antwerp, Kluwer, 1979, 245. These authors refer to an 'anticipating interpretation'.

43 M. VAN HOECKE, *De interpretatievrijheid van de rechter*, Antwerp, Kluwer, 1979, 248.

44 M. VAN HOECKE, *De interpretatievrijheid van de rechter*, Antwerp, Kluwer, 1979, 147.

45 P. DELNOY, *Eléments de méthodologie juridique*, Brussels, Larcier, 2008, 168; M. VAN HOECKE, *De interpretatievrijheid van de rechter*, Antwer, Kluwer, 1979, 148. See also:.M. POLAK, *Theorie en practijk der rechtsvinding*, Zwolle, W.E.J. Tjeenk Willink, 1953, 29.

46 P. DELNOY, *Eléments de méthodologie juridique*, Brussels, Larcier, 2008, 168.

47 F.T. GROENEWEGEN, *Wetsinterpretatie en rechtsvorming*, The Hague, Boom Juridische uitgevers, 2006, 147. See also: M. VAN HOECKE, *De interpretatievrijheid van de rechter*, Antwerp, Kluwer, 1979, 156–157.

workers' wages and salaries[48] and in the Belgian Act on employment contracts.[49] However, in both acts it has a different meaning.

Finally, the coherence and structure of a legal system can be affected by subsequent changes.[50] Very often the established framework of a legal system stays the same, although old provisions are abolished and new rules are introduced.[51] This might harm the structure of a legal system and can therefore hamper a systematic interpretation.[52]

3.1.3.4 Legal-historical interpretation

With a legal-historical interpretation legal scholars interpret legal provisions by considering their story of development. In order to sketch the *legal* history of a provision, researchers can look for previous versions in legislation or case law[53]: did the original provision change drastically or not?[54] Preparatory works will be an interesting source of information, as they discuss the problems and underlying reasons that led to the enactment or alternation of a provision.[55] Also subsequent preparatory works, court judgments or legal doctrine can provide (additional or more extensive) information on the development of existing law.[56] For example, in 1842 the Belgian compensatory interests were established by the Belgian Court of Cassation, regardless of any legislative initiative.[57] The considerations of the 1842 court judgment will therefore be of utmost importance for a legal-historical interpretation.

In order to sketch the *historical* background, legal scholars will search for historical events (e.g. the French Revolution) that led to the legal provisions under consideration.[58] These events are not always easy to determine.[59] However,

48 Belgian Act 12 April 1965 on the protection of workers' wages and salaries, *Belgian Bulletin of Acts* 30 april 1965.

49 Belgian Act of 3 July 1978 on employment contracts, *Belgian Bulletin of Acts* 22 augustus 1978.

50 M. VAN HOECKE, *De interpretatievrijheid van de rechter*, Antwerp, Kluwer, 1979, 158.

51 P. DELNOY, *Eléments de méthodologie juridique*, Brussels, Larcier, 2008, 169.

52 See also J. BELL and G. ENGLE, *Cross: Statutory Interpretation*, London, Butterworths, 1995, 150.

53 M. VAN HOECKE, *De interpretatievrijheid van de rechter*, Antwerp, Kluwer, 1979, 238; E. EGGERMONT, M. GEUNENS, F. GOWIE and E. TIMBERMONT, *Het juridisch verwerkingsproces*, Bruges, die Keure, 2014, 126.

54 M. VAN HOECKE, *De interpretatievrijheid van de rechter*, Antwerp, Kluwer, 1979, 251–252.

55 E. EGGERMONT, M. GEUENS, F. GOWIE and E. TIMBERMONT, *Het juridisch verwerkingsproces*, Bruges, die Keure, 2014, 126.

56 F.T. GROENEWEGEN, *Wetsinterpretatie en rechtsvorming*, The Hague, Boom Juridische uitgevers, 2006, 123.

57 As counterparts of the moratory interests in article 1153 Belgian Code civil. See: L. KESTEMONT, *Ockhams scheermes in het leerstuk van de Belgische nalatigheidsinteresten* (I. SAMOY and S. STIJNS, eds.), Bruges, die Keure, 2012, 2.

58 P. DELNOY, *Eléments de méthodologie juridique*, Brussels, Larcier, 2008, 171; M. VAN HOECKE, *De interpretatievrijheid van de rechter*, Antwerp, Kluwer, 1979, 236.

59 P. DELNOY, *Eléments de méthodologie juridique*, Brussels, Larcier, 2008, 174.

legal scholars can rely on existing (legal-)historical studies.[60] In that case, the legal research will become multi- or interdisciplinary.

When opting for a legal-historical interpretation some caution needs to be exercised. First of all, preparatory works only give a random indication of the generally received opinion at a specific moment in time.[61] The reasons why a legal provision was developed or altered may not only be superseded, but may even have disappeared due to legal, societal and/or economic developments. Second, it is possible that the meaning and the scope of words (both in common parlance and legal-technical) have evolved over time.[62]

3.1.3.5 Teleological interpretation

A teleological interpretation interprets a legal provision in view of the legislator's original objective(s): protecting specific interests, obtaining a particular social or economic outcome, stimulating a specific type of behaviour, etc.[63] Sometimes the legislation itself refers to its main objectives, for example in considerations prefacing the legislation (preambules).[64] However, as this is not always the case, preparatory works prove to be of significant value when applying a teleological interpretation. They reflect the procedure of developing legislation and consist of "bills, amendments, explanatory memoranda, reports to the King, reports of Senate and Chambers Commissions, reports of discussions in both Houses etc."[65]

Preparatory works allow to uncover the legislator's objectives rather quickly, including the underlying policies.[66] They clarify, for example, which (social) interests were preferable to others.[67] A legal scholar can also use interpretative

---

60 P. DELNOY, *Eléments de méthodologie juridique*, Brussels, Larcier, 2008, 195.

61 F.T. GROENEWEGEN, *Wetsinterpretatie en rechtsvorming*, The Hague, Boom Juridische uitgevers, 2006, 105.

62 P. DELNOY, *Eléments de méthodologie juridique*, Brussels, Larcier, 2008, 174.

63 P. DELNOY, *Eléments de méthodologie juridique*, Brussels, Larcier, 2008, 175–176; F.T. GROENEWEGEN, *Wetsinterpretatie en rechtsvorming*, The Hague, Boom Juridische uitgevers, 2006, 167.

64 A. PECZENIK, "Scientia Juris. Legal Doctrine as knowledge of Law and as a Source of Law" in E. PATTARO (ed.), *A Treatise of Legal Philosopy and General Jurisprudence*, Dordrecht, Springer, 2005, 24; F.T. GROENEWEGEN, *Wetsinterpretatie en rechtsvorming*, The Hague, Boom Juridische uitgevers, 2006, 170; J.M. POLAK, *Theorie en practijk der rechtsvinding*, Zwolle, W.E.J. Tjeenk Willink, 1953, 43.

65 Translation of: "wetsontwerpen, wetsvoorstellen, amendementen, memories van toelichting, verslagen aan de koning, rapporten, van senaats- en kamercommissies, diskussies in de kaders, e.d." M. VAN HOECKE, *De interpretatievrijheid van de rechter*, Antwerp, Kluwer, 1979, 202–203.

66 E. EGGERMONT, M. GEUNENS, F. GOWIE and E. TIMBERMONT, *Het juridisch verwerkingsproces*, Bruges, die Keure, 2014, 126; M. HERWEIJER, "Normen en rechtshandelingen. Rechtswetenschap als interpreteren en observeren" in J.W.L. BROEKSTEEG and E.F. STAMHUIS (eds.), *Rechtswetenschappelijk onderzoek. Over object en methode*, The Hague, Boom Juridische uitgevers, 2003, 28.

67 M. VAN HOECKE, *De interpretatievrijheid van de rechter*, Antwerp, Kluwer, 1979, 254 en 318.

laws clarifying the objectives of previous legislation.[68] It is, however, possible that those laws deviate from the original objectives due to legal, societal or economic circumstances.[69]

A teleological interpretation carries some risks. First of all, it relies on the legislator's original objectives. By no means the researcher can put forward his/her own objectives while pretending these are the legislator's.[70] Second, 'the legislator' is not just one person, but embodies a gathering of individuals.[71] In this respect, it is possible that members of a legislative assembly agree to adopt the same bill, while pursuing distinct objectives.[72] In those cases, it is most feasible to uncover the *general* objectives or to search for *common* denominators.[73] Finally, it is possible that the legislator's original objectives are superseded in view of recent social developments.

3.1.3.6 Interpretation based on jurisprudence

An interpretation based on jurisprudence interprets legal provisions in view of the opinions of the judiciary which are expressed in their courts judgments and are applied in (case) law.[74] Both national, European and international case law can be used. An interpretation on the basis of jurisprudence is interesting in the case of general legal concepts or open norms, such as 'in the best interest of the child' or 'giving notice'. As judges have to apply these general concepts in concrete cases, they will give a specific meaning on them.[75] This meaning can of course evolve in light of societal changes.[76] Also courts judgments contra legem or judgments filling loopholes in the law demonstrate that interpretations based on jurisprudence can be very helpful.

When opting for an interpretation based on jurisprudence, a legal scholar should focus on the relationship between different (deviant) court judgments

---

68 F.T. GROENEWEGEN, *Wetsinterpretatie en rechtsvorming,* The Hague, Boom Juridische uitgevers, 2006, 123.

69 F.T. GROENEWEGEN, *Wetsinterpretatie en rechtsvorming,* The Hague, Boom Juridische uitgevers, 2006, 124.

70 G. DE GEEST, "Hoe maken we van de rechtswetenschap een volwaardige wetenschap?", *NJB* 2004, 63.

71 K. LARENZ, *Methodenlehre der Rechtswissenschaft*, Berlin, Springer, 1983, 314.

72 J. BELL and G. ENGLE, *Cross: Statutory Interpretation,* London, Butterworths, 1995, 24.

73 M. VAN HOECKE, *De interpretatievrijheid van de rechter,* Antwerp, Kluwer, 1979, 212.

74 Dictionary van Dale. See also: E. EGGERMONT, M. GEUENS, F. GOWIE and E. TIMBERMONT, *Het juridisch verwerkingsproces*, Bruges, die Keure, 2014, 128.

75 F. KUNNEMAN, *Rechtswetenschap,* Nijmegen, Ars Aequi Libri, 1991, 5; E. EGGERMONT, M. GEUENS, F. GOWIE and E. TIMBERMONT, *Het juridisch verwerkingsproces*, Bruges, die Keure, 2014, 128.

76 P.G. KORREL and O.W.M. KAMSTRA, *Sociaal wetenschappelijke & juridische methodologie*, Amsterdam, Melkman, 1991, 53; E. EGGERMONT, M. GEUENS, F. GOWIE and E. TIMBERMONT, *Het juridisch verwerkingsproces*, Bruges, die Keure, 2014, 129.

and their reasoning.[77] Also precedents are of significance. Although only formally binding in common-law countries, precedents are also important to continental legal systems.[78] After all, judges of lower courts tend to apply rulings of higher courts in order to avoid a revocation later on.[79] In this respect, precedents contribute to the unity and to the legal certainty of a legal system.[80]

3.1.3.7 *Interpretation based on legal doctrine*

An interpretation based on legal doctrine interprets legal provisions in view of national, European and international literature.[81] This kind of interpretation is interesting when both legislation and case law are unclear, or when there seems to be an inconsistency between legal rules and their application by judges. Moreover, legal doctrine also contributes to the development, content and alteration of a legal system.[82]

3.1.3.8 *Interpretation based on non-binding legal sources*

A legal system is not only shaped by legislation, case law and legal doctrine. Also other (national, European, international) sources and institutions can leave their mark on the (functioning of a) legal system. Examples are: recommendations of the European Commission, national circulars, advices of privacy commissions, etc.[83] Legal scholars can use such non-binding legal sources in order to understand and interpret legal constructs. Their legal value and scope (in the case of a conflict with binding legal sources) can of course be debated.[84]

---

77 F. KUNNEMAN, *Rechtswetenschap*, Nijmegen, Ars Aequi Libri, 1991, 6–8.

78 A. PECZENIK, "Scientia Juris. Legal Doctrine as knowledge of Law and as a Source of Law" in E. PATTARO (ed.), *A Treatise of Legal Philosophy and General Jurisprudence*, Dordrecht, Springer, 2005, 25. For the use of predecents both in common law and continental legal systems, see i.a. R.S. SUMMERS and M. TARUFFO, "Interpretation and Comparative Analysis" in D.N. MACCORMICK and R.S. SUMMERS (eds.), Interpreting Statutes, Aldershot, Dartmouth, 1991, 487–490.

79 E. EGGERMONT, M. GEUENS, F. GOWIE and E. TIMBERMONT, *Het juridisch verwerkingsproces*, Bruges, die Keure, 2014, 128.

80 H. FRANKEN, *Encyclopedie van de rechtswetenschap,* Deventer, Gouda Quint, 2001, 199; G.A.F.M. VAN SCHAAIJK, *Praktijkgericht juridisch onderzoek*, The Hague, Boom Juridische uitgevers, 2011, 107.

81 E. EGGERMONT, M. GEUENS, F. GOWIE and E. TIMBERMONT, *Het juridisch verwerkingsproces*, Bruges, die Keure, 2014, 132.

82 E. EGGERMONT, M. GEUENS, F. GOWIE and E. TIMBERMONT, *Het juridisch verwerkingsproces*, Bruges, die Keure, 2014, 133.

83 J.B.M. VRANKEN, "Algemeen Deel. Een synthese" in *Mr. C. Assers Handleiding tot de beoefening van het Nederlands Burgerlijk Recht*, Deventer, Kluwer, 2014, 143.

84 J.B.M. VRANKEN, "Algemeen Deel. Een synthese" in *Mr. C. Assers Handleiding tot de beoefening van het Nederlands Burgerlijk Recht*, Deventer, Kluwer, 2014, 143.

3.1.3.9 Sociological interpretation

A sociological interpretation either interprets legal provisions in light of the social context that led to their enactment or in light of their present-day (possibly evolved) social context.[85] 'Social context' has a broad meaning, including prevailing ideologies, culture, specific social needs, etc.[86]

The first option focuses on the original social context that led to the creation or alteration of a legal construct. Preparatory works of legislation can be interesting to consult, as they often refer to the social motives(s) to create or alter a legal arrangement. These motives will often be supported by empirical studies (such as surveys and statistics) or other sociological research.[87] When looking into these studies, the research will get a multi- or interdisciplinary character.

In the second option, the focus is on the present-day social context, which evolves over time. For example, a legal provision containing the word group 'members of the family'. Decades ago, this word group would only cover 'a married man and woman with children born in wedlock.' However, a sociological interpretation in view of the present-day social context could broaden the scope to cohabiting partners, blended families, same-sex couples, etc. This kind of interpretation allows for legal provisions to evolve in light of modern social needs without having to formally alter legislation.[88]

3.1.4 INTERPRETATION AND NORMATIVE CHOICES

Legal scholars often interpret rules unconsciously.[89] Even when multiple interpretations are possible, legal scholars are not always aware of the fact that they make or have made a *choice*. For example, when the original objective of the legislator seems to be superseded, legal scholars almost automatically opt for a sociological interpretation.[90] It is also true that after some time the meaning and scope of a legal rule can become self-evident, because all legal actors (legislators, judges, researchers) interpret it in the same way. According to VAN

85 P. DELNOY, *Eléments de méthodologie juridique*, Brussels, Larcier, 2008, 178.

86 P. DELNOY, *Eléments de méthodologie juridique*, Brussels, Larcier, 2008, 178.

87 P. DELNOY, *Eléments de méthodologie juridique*, Brussels, Larcier, 2008, 195.

88 M. VAN HOECKE, *Is de rechtswetenschap een empirische wetenschap?*, The Hague, Boom Juridische uitgevers, 2010, 20; R. KRANENBURG, *De grondslagen der rechtswetenschap*, Haarlem, Tjeenk Willink, 1952, 32; G.A.F.M. VAN SCHAAIJK, *Praktijkgericht juridisch onderzoek*, The Hague, Boom Juridische uitgevers, 2011, 108; P. VAN BEMMELEN, *Regtsgeleerde opstellen*, I, Leiden, E.J. Brill, 1891, 5; J.M. POLAK, *Theorie en practijk der rechtsvinding*, Zwolle, W.E.J. Tjeenk Willink, 1953, 45.

89 M. VAN HOECKE, "Aard en methode van de rechtsdogmatiek", *R & R* 1984, 191.

90 F.T. GROENEWEGEN, *Wetsinterpretatie en rechtsvorming*, The Hague, Boom Juridische uitgevers, 2006, 175.

HOECKE, there is even a "minimal consensus on the meaning of most legal texts."[91]

Despite this "minimal consensus" on the meaning of most legal rules, the meaning of other rules can still be under discussion. After all, legal scholars can choose from a wide range of different interpretations, all having their own focus and therefore (possibly) leading to a different outcome.[92] It is up to the researcher to decide which interpretation is given priority[93], implying a consideration and a choice.[94] The researcher will therefore make a normative value judgment on how a legal provision should be interpreted: what is its optimal or desirable meaning?[95] Concealing the preferred interpretation as an 'objective' description of the law is unacceptable.[96] Researchers have to clarify on the basis of which arguments and types of interpretation they have made their choice.[97] Also the description angle will play a role.

The line between 'describing' and 'deciding which interpretation is desirable' is rather thin.[98] This is because legal scholars always want to improve the law.[99] RUBIN expresses this aptly by means of a comparison between literary criticism and legal scholarship:

---

91 M. VAN HOECKE, *Is de rechtswetenschap een empirische wetenschap?*, The Hague, Boom Juridische uitgevers, 2010, 19; M. VAN HOECKE, "Legal Doctrine: Which Method(s) for What Kind of Discipline?" in M. VAN HOECKE (ed.), *Methodologies of Legal Research*, Oxford, Hart Publishing, 2011, 13.

92 M. VAN HOECKE, "Aard en methode van de rechtsdogmatiek", *R & R* 1984, 192.

93 P.W. KAMPHUISEN, *Beschouwingen over rechtswetenschap*, Nijmegen, Dekker & Van De Vegt, 1938, 61; J. VRANKEN, "Wij weten wel wat wij doen. Over juridisch-dogmatisch onderzoek in het privaatrecht, maar wel een slag anders", *NJB* 2014, 1734.

94 J.B.M. VRANKEN, "Algemeen Deel. Een synthese" in *Mr. C. Assers Handleiding tot de beoefening van het Nederlands Burgerlijk Recht*, Deventer, Kluwer, 2014, 136.

95 M. VAN HOECKE, "Aard en methode van de rechtsdogmatiek", *R & R* 1984, 192; J.M. SMITS, *The Mind and Method of the Legal Academic,* Cheltenham, Edward Elgar, 2012, 14 and 43; C.E. SMITH, W. GEELHOED, M.J. DUBELAAR, B.P. TER HAAR, J. VAN RIJN VAN ALKEMADE, K. VAN WILLIGENBURG, A. SPRANGERS, J. VAN RIJN, T. ELSEMAN, A. BOGAERTS, S. DE GOEDE, J. ALSEMGEEST, A. BOGAERTS, S. KOUSEDGHI, and E. VAN DER DEIJL, "Criteria voor goed rechtswetenschappelijk onderzoek. De omgekeerde route", *NJB* 2008, 686; A. PECZENIK, "Scientia Juris. Legal Doctrine as knowledge of Law and as a Source of Law" in E. PATTARO (ed.), *A Treatise of Legal Philosophy and General Jurisprudence,* Dordrecht, Springer, 2005, 4; J.M. SMITS, *The Mind and Method of the Legal Academic,* Cheltenham, Edward Elgar, 2012, 18; S. PIMONT, "À propos de l'activité doctrinale civiliste", *RTDCiv.* 2006, 712.

96 G. DE GEEST, "Hoe maken we van de rechtswetenschap een volwaardige wetenschap?", *NJB* 2004, 63; J.M. SMITS, *The Mind and Method of the Legal Academic,* Cheltenham, Edward Elgar, 2012, 43; W.H. VAN BOOM, "Empirisch privaatrecht: enige beschouwingen over de rol van empirisch onderzoek in de hedendaagse privaatrechtswetenschap", *TPR* 2013, 13.

97 J.B.M. VRANKEN, "Als een arrest niet bevalt, laten wij het gewoon weg" in H. NIEUWENHUIS (ed.), *Ex Libris*, Deventer, Kluwer, 2009, 90.

98 A. PECZENIK, "Scientia Juris. Legal Doctrine as knowledge of Law and as a Source of Law" in E. PATTARO (ed.), *A Treatise of Legal Philosophy and General Jurisprudence,* Dordrecht, Springer, 2005, 4. Some authors are even of the opinion that every interpretation holds a normative value judgment. See: C. SMITH, "Het normatieve karakter van de rechtswetenschap: recht als oordeel", *R & R* 2009, 202–225; A. SOETEMAN, "Wetenschappelijke rechtsgeleerdheid", *R & R* 2009, 226–235.

99 E.L. RUBIN, "Law and the Methodology of Law", *Wis.L.Rev.* 1997, 530.

> "In essence, they [literary critics] regard the author as a person of genius perhaps, or talent at least, whose work they are in a position to interpret and evaluate, but not improve. [...] Deep down inside, legal scholars tend to think that they could do a better job than the judge. Thus, their interpretive efforts to determine the meaning of a particular opinion are often preliminary to prescriptive statements that evaluate the desirability of the determined meaning."[100]

Nevertheless, legal scholars should be aware that when they are deciding on how a legal rule *should* be interpreted, they are not simply 'describing' the law.[101]

In the past legal research was nationally oriented and monodisciplinary in a sense that it was both carried out and read by researchers/practitioners from the same national context and legal discipline. However, due to internationalization and the rise of multi- and interdisciplinary research, the context has changed. Legal scholars are now encouraged to publish their work in international journals and to collaborate with other academic disciplines. This wider range of legal research leads to a more diverse reading public. As a consequence, authors and readers do no longer belong to the same national context or the same academic discipline, in which there is a 'minimal consensus on the meaning of most legal texts.' Also this change of context should incite legal scholars to become more aware and more explicit about their interpretation of the law, and the choices they have made in this matter.

3.2 METHODOLOGICAL FEATURES OF A CLASSIFYING RESEARCH OBJECTIVE

A classifying research objective aims to conceptualize or classify (legal) phenomena in the existing legal system. In this section we discuss the classification angle, the classification criteria and the classification process.

3.2.1 CLASSIFICATION ANGLE

Legal scholars have to make the sources for their classification explicit, as they determine the angle of the classification.[102] Firstly, *internal sources of the national legal system* can be used[103]: national legislation, customary law, general

100 E.L. RUBIN, "Law and the Methodology of Law", *Wis.L.Rev.* 1997, 530.

101 M. VAN HOECKE, *Inleiding tot het recht. Rechtstheorie. Deel 2,* Brussels, UFSAL Brussels, 1988, 260.

102 J.M. SMITS, *The Mind and Method of the Legal Academic,* Cheltenham, Edward Elgar, 2012, 116.

103 M. VAN HOECKE, "Hoe wetenschappelijk is de rechtswetenschap?", *TPR* 2009, 657–663; C. MCCRUDDEN, "Legal Research and the Social Sciences", *L.Q.R.* 2006, 634; R.A.

principles, etc. Not the historical, sociological or ethical background, but "the inner consistency of the whole system" will play a role for the classification.[104]

Secondly, in a context of internationalization and globalization the plurality of legal systems has increased.[105] In that respect, a classification can also use *internal sources of the international legal community.* For areas of law in which the international community frequently enacts legislation, this might even be essential.

Finally, a classification can also take into account knowledge from other academic disciplines. In that case, legal scholars use *external sources from other academic disciplines,* such as social sciences.[106] Also insights from history, philosophy and political sciences can be used in order to broaden the classification angle.[107] In these cases, the traditional legal research gets a multi- or interdisciplinary character.

3.2.2 CLASSIFICATION CRITERIA

A classification "divides objects into various groups according to their common characteristics and their differences."[108] For that purpose, legal scholars should clarify their classification criteria."[109] After all, whether or not two legal constructs belong to the same category will always depend on the criteria that the researcher puts forward as being "decisive" for the classification.[110] When

EPSTEIN, "Let 'The Fundamental Things Apply': Necessary and Contingent Truths in Legal Scholarship", *Harv.L.Rev.* 2002, 1298.

104 H.U. KANTOROWICZ and E.W. PATTERSON, "Legal Science – A Summary of Its Methodology", *Colum.L.Rev.* 1928, 688.

105 M. VAN HOECKE, "Hoe wetenschappelijk is de rechtswetenschap?", *TPR* 2009, 659; C. MCCRUDDEN, "Legal Research and the Social Sciences", *L.Q.R.* 2006, 644; J.-L HALPÉRIN, "Law in books and law in action: the problem of legal change", *Me.L.Rev.* 2011–2012, 69.

106 See: M. VAN HOECKE, "Hoe wetenschappelijk is de rechtswetenschap?", *TPR* 2009, 662.

107 L. KESTEMONT, *Naar een rechtswetenschappelijke methodeleer. Een expliciet methodologisch kader voor rechtswetenschappelijk onderzoek in het socialezekerheidsrecht,* Bruges, die Keure (reeks Begasoz/ Abetrass), 2017, 134.

108 Translation of "[...] verdeelt de kenobjecten in onderscheiden groepen naar hun gemeenschappelijke karaktertrekken en naar hun verschillen [...]." P.W. KAMPHUISEN, *Beschouwingen over rechtswetenschap,* Nijmegen, Dekker & Van De Vegt, 1938, 70. See also: J.M. POLAK, *Theorie en practijk der rechtsvinding,* Zwolle, W.E.J. Tjeenk Willink, 1953, 31–32.

109 "The focal point of classification": G. SAMUEL, *Epistemology and Method in Law,* Aldershot, Ashgate, 2003, 219.

110 The concept 'decisive criteria' was adopted from PINTENS' *Inleiding tot de rechtsvergelijking* from 1998. He uses the concept in the context of a comparative law study looking for 'typical solutions' in order to come to a typology of legal systems on the basis of a 'decisive criterion'. See: W. PINTENS, *Inleiding tot de rechtsvergelijking,* Leuven, Universitaire Pers Leuven, 1998, 86. Also other authors refer to the importance of criteria when classifying legal families: e.g. N. JANSEN, "Comparative Law and Comparative Knowledge" in M. REIMANN and R. ZIMMERMANN (eds.), *The Oxford Handbook of Comparative Law,* Oxford, Oxford

deciding on classification criteria, the classification angle that was chosen by the researcher will play a significant role.[111]

Legal scholars can put forward their own classification criteria, or they can derive existing criteria from legislation, case law or legal doctrine.[112] After all, also legislators, judges and other legal authors deal with classification issues and decide on classification criteria. Legal scholars can decide to use them and to go along with an existing discourse, already developed by others. Or they can put forward their own selection of criteria.

Classification criteria can be quite diverse, focusing on legal modalities (e.g. formalities), underlying legal principles, objectives of legislation, relationships between parties, types of damages, damaged objects, etc.[113] The selected criteria will enlarge some differences and consider other to be irrelevant.[114] Moreover, a lesser amount of criteria leads to a larger amount of classification possibilities. If for example 'sharing the same objective' is a classification criterion, all legal constructs with the same objective fall under the same category. If on the other hand, two criteria are used (e.g. 'sharing the same objective' and 'sharing the same formalities'), the number of legal constructs within one category will be much less.

As the selected criteria are decisive for the classification, legal scholars have to make them explicit. This allows for readers to assess the classification. Moreover, explicit classification criteria are important in light of future evolutions: throughout time some criteria can become more important, whereas other lose their value. This may lead to a reconsideration of existing classifications. VAN HOECKE presents the following example: "If the legislator would introduce e.g. a 'company with social purpose' and would remove the profit motive as an essential constituent of a company, this would lead to a serious shaking of the traditional corporate law system as the distinction between a 'company' and an 'organization' had until then always been based on the presence or absence of a profit motive."[115]

University Press, 2006, 317; C. VALCKE, "Reflections on comparative law methodology – getting inside contract law" in M. ADAMS and J. BOMHOFF (eds.), *Practice and Theory in Comparative Law*, Cambridge, Cambridge University Press, 2012, 45.

111 F. KUNNEMAN, *Rechtswetenschap*, Nijmegen, Ars Aequi Libri, 1991, 4.

112 L. KESTEMONT, *Naar een rechtswetenschappelijke methodeleer. Een expliciet methodologisch kader voor rechtswetenschappelijk onderzoek in het socialezekerheidsrecht*, Bruges, die Keure (reeks Begasoz/ Abetrass), 2017, 194.

113 G. SAMUEL, *Epistemology and Method in Law*, Aldershot, Ashgate, 2003, 221.

114 M. VAN HOECKE, *Is de rechtswetenschap een empirische wetenschap?*, The Hague, Boom Juridische uitgevers, 2010, 27.

115 Translation of: "Wanneer de wetgever bv. de "vennootschap met sociaal oogmerk" invoert en het winstoogmerk schrapt als constitutief bestanddeel van een vennootschap leidt dit tot een grondig door elkaar schudden van de klassieke systematiek van het rechtspersonenrecht, waar het onderscheid tussen "vennootschap" en "vereniging" tot dan precies gesteund was op de aan- resp. afwezigheid van het winstoogmerk." M. VAN HOECKE, "Hoe wetenschappelijk is de rechtswetenschap?", *TPR* 2009, 658.

3.2.3 CLASSIFICATION PROCESS

In order to classify, researchers will first describe the characteristics of the legal constructs and legal categories concerned. In a second step, the characteristics are compared.[116] The comparison will uncover mutual similarities and differences in light of the selected classification criteria.[117] This allows to assess in a final step under which category a legal construct can be ranged, which legal constructs belong to same category, which court judgments are reflecting the same legal doctrine, etc.

A clear set of classification criteria does, however, not guarantee that a legal scholar is able to range every legal construct under an existing legal category. After all, it is possible that its characteristics are so specific that it cannot be ranged under an existing category. This will probably lead to the rise of new legal categories.[118]

To end, when pursuing a classification it is important to make sure that the concepts and categorizations involved are always (i) simple and unambiguous, (ii) corresponding to reality and (iii) functional from a legal perspective.[119]

3.3 METHODOLOGICAL FEATURES OF A COMPARATIVE RESEARCH OBJECTIVE

Legal provisions and arrangements can be compared internally (within the same legal system), historically (different periods in time) and externally (different present-day legal systems). This section focuses on the methodological features of external comparison, as thoroughly discussed in literature. However, most of these features apply to internal and historical comparison as they also concern a comparison of two or more legal constructs or systems.

We will first look into six general methodological features: the reasons to compare, the nature of the comparison (micro/macro), the *tertium comparationis*, the choice of legal systems, the access to sources and the approach of the comparison (dogmatic, functional, *sui generis*). Afterwards we discuss the different stages of the comparison process: (i) describing the legal systems, (ii) comparing the legal systems, (iii) explaining the uncovered similarities and differences, and (iv) evaluating the results of the comparison.

---

116 See also: M. ADAMS, "Controlled Comparison and Language of Description" in M. ADAMS and D. HEIRBAUT (eds.), *The Method and Methodology of Comparative Law. Essays in Honour of Mark Van Hoecke*, Oxford, Hart Publishing, 2014, 88.

117 J.M. FEINMAN, "The Jurisprudence of Classification", *Stan.L.Rev.* 1989, 674. See also: G.A.F.M. VAN SCHAAIJK, *Praktijkgericht juridisch onderzoek*, The Hague, Boom Juridische uitgevers, 2011, 88.

118 L. KESTEMONT, *Naar een rechtswetenschappelijke methodeleer. Een expliciet methodologisch kader voor rechtswetenschappelijk onderzoek in het socialezekerheidsrecht*, Bruges, die Keure (reeks Begasoz/ Abetrass), 2017, 194.

119 L. KESTEMONT, *Naar een rechtswetenschappelijke methodeleer. Een expliciet methodologisch kader voor rechtswetenschappelijk onderzoek in het socialezekerheidsrecht*, Bruges, die Keure (reeks Begasoz/ Abetrass), 2017, 194.

3.3.1 GENERAL METHODOLOGICAL FEATURES

3.3.1.1 Reason(s) to compare

In legal scholarship comparative law is rather popular and is conducted for several reasons.[120] It is therefore important that legal scholars clarify *why* they decide to do a comparison.[121] After all, there is a difference between comparisons "used e.g. for harmonization in Europe, for ameliorating one's own legal system, for understanding or explaining differences between legal systems, or as argument in a court judgment or publication."[122]

The reason(s) to compare will have significant influence on the methodological choices before, during and after the actual comparison.[123] Reference can be made to the nature of the comparison (micro or macro), the choice of legal systems, the source material, the approach of the comparison, the evaluation of the comparison results, etc.[124] In other words: "the goal one pursues, the function of the comparison determines the road to follow, the methodology of comparison."[125]

3.3.1.2 Micro/macro comparison

Legal scholars can opt for a micro or macro comparison. Micro comparative law concentrates on specific legal constructs, problems and solutions in different legal systems.[126] Macro comparative law focuses on legal systems in their

120 J. HUSA, "Research Designs of Comparative Law – Methodology or Heuristics" in M. ADAMS and D. HEIRBAUT (eds.), *The Method and Culture of Comparative Law*, Oxford, Hart Publishing, 2014, 53.

121 J.B.M. VRANKEN, "Algemeen Deel. Een synthese" in *Mr. C. Assers Handleiding tot de beoefening van het Nederlands Burgerlijk Recht*, Deventer, Kluwer, 2014, 168.

122 Translation of: "wordt ingezet bijvoorbeeld voor de harmonisatie in Europa, voor een verbetering van het eigen recht, voor het begrijpen of verklaren van verschillen tussen rechtsstelsels dan wel als argument in een rechtelijke uitspraak of publicatie." J.B.M. VRANKEN, "Algemeen Deel. Een synthese" in *Mr. C. Assers Handleiding tot de beoefening van het Nederlands Burgerlijk Recht*, Deventer, Kluwer, 2014, 168.

123 D. PIETERS, "Functions of comparative law and practical methodology of comparing" in *Syllabus Research Master in Law*, Leuven-Tilburg, 2009, 23; C. MORRIS AND C. MURPHY, *Getting a PhD in Law*, Oxford, Hart Publishing, 2011, 38.

124 F.F. STONE, "The end to be served by comparative law", *Tul.L.Rev.* 1950–51, 333; D. PIETERS, "Functions of comparative law and practical methodology of comparing" in *Syllabus Research Master in Law*, Leuven-Tilburg, 2009, 1 en 14; W. DEVROE, *Rechtsvergelijking in een context van europeanisering en globalisering*, Leuven, Acco, 2010, 22.

125 D. PIETERS, "Functions of comparative law and practical methodology of comparing" in *Syllabus Research Master in Law*, Leuven-Tilburg, 2009, 23.

126 J. HUSA, "Research Designs of Comparative Law" in M. ADAMS and D. HEIRBAUT (eds.), *The Method and Methodology of Comparative Law. Essays in Honour of Mark Van Hoecke*, Oxford, Hart Publishing, 2014, 57; W. DEVROE, *Rechtsvergelijking in een context van europeanisering en globalisering*, Leuven, Acco, 2010, 32; G. DANNEMANN, "Comparative Law: Study of Similarities or Differences?" in M. REIMANN and R. ZIMMERMANN (eds.),

entirety: their structure and fundamental principles, but also "the spirit and style of different legal systems, the methods of thought and procedures they use."[127] Although legal scholars should consider in advance whether their comparisons will be of a micro or macro nature, it is possible that the comparative research is a mix of both.

3.3.1.3 *Tertium comparationis*

Every comparison requires a *tertium comparationis:* in order to compare legal constructs, those constructs need to have something in common.[128] For example: two legal constructs can share a common legal principle, can tackle the same social problem, can strive for the same objective, can have the same format or legal consequences etc.[129] It is of course possible to have multiple *tertia comparationis.*[130]

Knowing whether there is indeed a common characteristic between legal constructs requires some foreknowledge or even a preliminary study.[131] Also the

---

The Oxford Handbook of Comparative Law, Oxford, Oxford University Press, 2006, 387; K. ZWEIGERT and H. KÖTZ, *An Introduction to Comparative Law*, Oxford, Oxford University Press, 1997, 5; A.E. ODERKERK, *De preliminaire fase van het rechtsvergelijkend onderzoek*, Nijmegen, Ars Aequi Libri, 1999, 224; F. GORLÉ, G. BOURGEOIS, H. BOCKEN e.a., *Rechtsvergelijking*, Mechelen, Kluwer, 2007, 2.

127 K. ZWEIGERT and H. KÖTZ, *An Introduction to Comparative Law*, Oxford, Oxford University Press, 1997, 4. See also: A.E. ODERKERK, *De preliminaire fase van het rechtsvergelijkend onderzoek*, Nijmegen, Ars Aequi Libri, 1999, 224; J. HUSA, "Research Designs of Comparative Law" in M. ADAMS en D. HEIRBAUT (eds.), *The Method and Methodology of Comparative Law. Essays in Honour of Mark Van Hoecke*, Oxford, Hart Publishing, 2014, 57; W. DEVROE, *Rechtsvergelijking in een context van europeanisering en globalisering*, Leuven, Acco, 2010, 33; G. DANNEMANN, "Comparative Law: Study of Similarities or Differences?" in M. REIMANN and R. ZIMMERMANN (eds.), *The Oxford Handbook of Comparative Law*, Oxford, Oxford University Press, 2006, 387; F. GORLÉ, G. BOURGEOIS, H. BOCKEN e.a., *Rechtsvergelijking*, Mechelen, Kluwer, 2007, 2.

128 See A.E. ODERKERK, *De preliminaire fase van het rechtsvergelijkend onderzoek*, Nijmegen, Ars Aequi Libri, 1999, 63–67 (and references) en 234; W. DEVROE, *Rechtsvergelijking in een context van europeanisering en globalisering*, Leuven, Acco, 2010, 44; M. ADAMS, "Wat de rechtsvergelijking vermag", *AA* 2011, 200; M. SCHMITTHOFF, "The science of comparative law", *C.L.J.* 1939, 96; E. ÖRÜCÜ, "Developing Comparative Law" in E. ÖRÜCÜ and D. NELKEN (eds.), *Comparative* Law, Oxford, Hart Publishing, 2007, 48; J.B.M. VRANKEN, "Algemeen Deel. Een synthese" in *Mr. C. Assers Handleiding tot de beoefening van het Nederlands Burgerlijk Recht*, Deventer, Kluwer, 2014, 169.

129 J.C. REITZ, "How to Do Comparative Law?", *Am.J.Comp.L.* 1998, 622; W. PINTENS, *Inleiding tot de rechtsvergelijking*, Leuven, Universitaire Pers Leuven, 1998, 50; E. ÖRÜCÜ, "Developing Comparative Law" in E. ÖRÜCÜ and D. NELKEN (eds.), *Comparative* Law, Oxford, Hart Publishing, 2007, 48; A.E. ODERKERK, *De preliminaire fase van het rechtsvergelijkend onderzoek*, Nijmegen, Ars Aequi Libri, 1999, 63–67 (and references).

130 N. JANSEN, "Comparative Law and Comparative Knowledge" in M. REIMANN and R. ZIMMERMANN (eds.), *The Oxford Handbook of Comparative Law*, Oxford, Oxford University Press, 2006, 315.

131 M. ADAMS, "Controlled Comparison and Language of Description" in M. ADAMS and D. HEIRBAUT (eds.), *The Method and Methodology of Comparative Law. Essays in Honour of*

researcher's interests and the reason(s) to compare play a decisive role. In this respect JANSEN clarifies that:

> "tertia comparationis are not objectively 'in the air'; rather they result from a choice about 'what matters', that is, which aspects of the law are relevant for the comparative lawyer, and which aspects of the law might benefit from the additional knowledge which comparison provides."[132]

A meaningful comparison does not only require a *tertium comparationis,* but there also have to be enough differences between the legal constructs under comparison. After all, as DANNEMANN puts it aptly: "there is no point in comparing what is identical, and little point in comparing what has nothing in common." Two legal constructs can have the same format, but a different objective, or they can share the same objective, but in a different format.[133]

3.3.1.4 Choice of legal systems

The choice of legal systems depends on the research topic, the overall research project – of which the comparison is a part –, and the researcher's reason(s) to compare.[134] A research exploring the feasibility of an EU harmonization measure will most likely opt for a comparison between Member States that differ considerably, whereas a research searching for inspiration in order to solve a national problem will probably look for legal systems with a similar political and social-economic context.[135] The same is true for micro and macro comparison: macro comparisons often focus on legal systems of different legal families, whereas micro comparisons are more interested in legal systems of the same legal

Mark Van Hoecke, Oxford, Hart Publishing, 2014, 95; J. HUSA, "Farewell to Functionalism of Methodological Tolerance?", *The Rabel Journal of Comparative and International Private Law* 2003, 426; W. PINTENS, *Inleiding tot de rechtsvergelijking,* Leuven, Universitaire Pers Leuven, 1998, 50.

132 N. JANSEN, "Comparative Law and Comparative Knowledge" in M. REIMANN and R. ZIMMERMANN (eds.), *The Oxford Handbook of Comparative Law,* Oxford, Oxford University Press, 2006, 314.

133 A.E. ODERKERK, *De preliminaire fase van het rechtsvergelijkend onderzoek,* Nijmegen, Ars Aequi Libri, 1999, 234; See also J.C. REITZ, "How to Do Comparative Law?", *Am.J.Comp.L.* 1998, 622.

134 G. DANNEMANN, "Comparative Law: Study of Similarities or Differences?" in M. REIMANN and R. ZIMMERMANN (eds.), *The Oxford Handbook of Comparative Law,* Oxford, Oxford University Press, 2006, 409; K. ZWEIGERT and H. KÖTZ, *An Introduction to Comparative Law,* Oxford, Oxford University Press, 1997, 41; A.E. ODERKERK, *De preliminaire fase van het rechtsvergelijkend onderzoek,* Nijmegen, Ars Aequi Libri, 1999, 54–58 (see references) and 228; W. DEVROE, *Rechtsvergelijking in een context van europeanisering en globalisering,* Leuven, Acco, 2010, 43; F. GORLÉ, G. BOURGEOIS, H. BOCKEN et al, *Rechtsvergelijking,* Mechelen, Kluwer, 2007, 29.

135 See A.E. ODERKERK, *De preliminaire fase van het rechtsvergelijkend onderzoek,* Nijmegen, Ars Aequi Libri, 1999, 55–56 (and references).

family.[136] Other reasons for selecting a legal system can be: the deviant nature of a legal system, the fact that a matter is actually regulated in a legal system, the influence of a country on the decision-making process within the EU, etc.[137] It is always up to the legal scholars to explicitly motivate why they have chosen the legal systems.[138] The motivation can be of a positive nature (why were these legal systems chosen? why is the proposed combination of legal systems interesting?) or a negative one (why were other legal systems excluded?).

In order to make a well-considered choice, the researcher will have to conduct a preliminary study.[139] Such preparatory studies avoid that the chosen legal systems lead to a useless or irrelevant result in the end. Both *tertia comparationis* and existing differences will be decisive for the selection.[140]

The number of legal systems involved in a comparison might differ. Some authors advise including as many systems as possible[141], whereas others consider a comparison of three legal systems to be standard.[142] As it is always uncertain how much time a researcher will spend on comparing legal systems, the number of systems should be a well-considered, and not too optimistic choice.[143] In the end, also this choice will depend on the research topic, the reason(s) to compare and the nature of the comparison (micro v macro).[144]

Finally, language knowledge of researchers might play a role when deciding on the legal systems to compare.[145] If indeed this is the case, researchers have to

---

136 D. PIETERS, "Functions of comparative law and practical methodology of comparing" in *Syllabus Research Master in Law*, Leuven-Tilburg, 2009, 15.

137 L. KESTEMONT, *Naar een rechtswetenschappelijke methodeleer. Een expliciet methodologisch kader voor rechtswetenschappelijk onderzoek in het socialezekerheidsrecht*, Bruges, die Keure (reeks Begasoz/ Abetrass), 2017, 196.

138 H. TIJSSEN, *De juridische dissertatie onder de loep*, The Hague, Boom Juridische uitgevers, 2009, 77.

139 A.E. ODERKERK, *De preliminaire fase van het rechtsvergelijkend onderzoek*, Nijmegen, Ars Aequi Libri, 1999, 52–53 (and references); F. GORLÉ, G. BOURGEOIS, H. BOCKEN et al, *Rechtsvergelijking*, Mechelen, Kluwer, 2007, 30; W. DEVROE, *Rechtsvergelijking in een context van europeanisering en globalisering*, Leuven, Acco, 2010, 43; J.B.M. VRANKEN, "Algemeen Deel. Een synthese" in *Mr. C. Assers Handleiding tot de beoefening van het Nederlands Burgerlijk Recht*, Deventer, Kluwer, 2014, 170.

140 DANNEMANN stresses *"a minimum of difference between the systems under consideration to make a comparative enquiry worthwile"*. See G. DANNEMANN, "Comparative Law: Study of Similarities or Differences?" in M. REIMANN and R. ZIMMERMANN (eds.), *The Oxford Handbook of Comparative Law*, Oxford, Oxford University Press, 2006, 409.

141 D. PIETERS, "Functions of comparative law and practical methodology of comparing" in *Syllabus Research Master in Law*, Leuven-Tilburg, 2009, 16. Especially in view of an evaluation later on in the research: See M. SCHMITTHOFF, "The science of comparative law", *C.L.J.* 1939, 97.

142 See M. SIEMS, *Comparative Law*, Cambridge, Cambridge University Press, 2014, 15.

143 W. DEVROE, *Inleiding tot de rechtsvergelijking*, Leuven, Acco, 2006, 14; M. SALTER and J. MASON, *Writing Law Dissertations*, Essex, Pearson, 2007, 189.

144 D. PIETERS, "Functions of comparative law and practical methodology of comparing" in *Syllabus Research Master in Law*, Leuven-Tilburg, 2009, 16.

145 J.B.M. VRANKEN, "Algemeen Deel. Een synthese" in *Mr. C. Assers Handleiding tot de beoefening van het Nederlands Burgerlijk Recht*, Deventer, Kluwer, 2014, 170.

explicitly mention it.[146] This way the reader knows that some legal systems are not a part of the comparison because of personal/subjective reasons. However, a lack of language knowledge may never lead to an uninteresting or useless comparison. There have to be sufficient objective reasons to justify the choice of legal systems.

3.3.1.5 Access to sources

Access to sufficient, liable, meticulous and up-to-date sources is vital for every comparison.[147] Authors also stress the use of primary or original sources.[148] However, if legal scholars do not master the foreign language, they can make use of secondary sources. Examples are: translations of legal texts, annotations of foreign case law, existing comparative legal research, etc. In this respect, *national* secondary sources made for *internal* use are relatively the safest option.[149] However, attentiveness is still required. After all, every translation is the result of an interpretation by the translator.[150] Also when using results of an existing comparative study, researchers should be aware that each study is conducted from a specific angle, determined by the research topic, the reason(s) for comparison, its limitations etc.[151] In order to obtain reliable information, legal scholars should consult multiple secondary sources and should determine their quality.[152] In case of doubt or contradiction between the consulted sources, it is possible to ask for help from local experts.[153]

---

146 A.E. ODERKERK, *De preliminaire fase van het rechtsvergelijkend onderzoek*, Nijmegen, Ars Aequi Libri, 1999, 231; R. VAN GESTEL, H.-W. MICKLITZ AND M. POIARES MADURO, "Methodology in the New Legal World", *Department of Law EUI Working Papers*, 2012/13, 23.

147 D. PIETERS, "Functions of comparative law and practical methodology of comparing" in *Syllabus Research Master in Law*, Leuven-Tilburg, 2009, 16–18; W. DEVROE, *Rechtsvergelijking in een context van europeanisering en globalisering*, Leuven, Acco, 2010, 48.

148 W. DEVROE, *Rechtsvergelijking in een context van europeanisering en globalisering*, Leuven, Acco, 2010, 48; D. PIETERS, "Functions of comparative law and practical methodology of comparing" in *Syllabus Research Master in Law*, Leuven-Tilburg, 2009, 20; W. PINTENS, *Inleiding tot de rechtsvergelijking*, Leuven, Universitaire Pers Leuven, 1998, 50; F. GORLÉ, G. BOURGEOIS, H. BOCKEN et al, *Rechtsvergelijking*, Mechelen, Kluwer, 2007, 38; J.B.M. VRANKEN, "Algemeen Deel. Een synthese" in *Mr. C. Assers Handleiding tot de beoefening van het Nederlands Burgerlijk Recht*, Deventer, Kluwer, 2014, 170.

149 D. PIETERS, "Functions of comparative law and practical methodology of comparing" in *Syllabus Research Master in Law*, Leuven-Tilburg, 2009, 20.

150 R.A.J. VAN GESTEL and J.B.M. VRANKEN, "Rechtswetenschappelijke artikelen", *NJB* 2007, 1456; D. PIETERS, "Functions of comparative law and practical methodology of comparing" in *Syllabus Research Master in Law*, Leuven-Tilburg, 2009, 20; C. MORRIS and C. MURPHY, *Getting a PhD in Law*, Oxford, Hart Publishing, 2011, 38; J.B.M. VRANKEN, "Algemeen Deel. Een synthese" in *Mr. C. Assers Handleiding tot de beoefening van het Nederlands Burgerlijk Recht*, Deventer, Kluwer, 2014, 114.

151 D. PIETERS, "Functions of comparative law and practical methodology of comparing" in *Syllabus Research Master in Law*, Leuven-Tilburg, 2009, 18–19.

152 W. DEVROE, *Rechtsvergelijking in een context van europeanisering en globalisering*, Leuven, Acco, 2010, 50; J.C. REITZ, "How to Do Comparative Law?", *Am.J.Comp.L.* 1998, 633.

153 D. PIETERS, "Functions of comparative law and practical methodology of comparing" in *Syllabus Research Master in Law*, Leuven-Tilburg, 2009, 22; W. PINTENS, *Inleiding*

Legal scholars should be transparent about their use of sources. If, for example, only case law of the highest courts was consulted, this has to be explicitly mentioned. After all, case law of a country's highest court is not always representative for its lower courts.[154] Moreover, it is also important to consult the same type of sources for each legal system. A researcher cannot consider legislation, case law and legal doctrine for one legal system, and only legislation for the others.[155] This would lead to an unbalanced description and comparison of the legal systems involved.

3.3.1.6 Comparison approach

Legal scholars can use different approaches in order to compare legal systems. Most famous are the dogmatic and the functional approach of comparative law. There is a marked preference for the functional approach, as in certain ways it meets the difficulties encountered by the dogmatic approach. Although the functional approach is also subject to criticism[156], it is difficult to come up with a better alternative and therefore it remains popular.[157] Nonetheless, the functional approach is not the only way to conduct comparative law and cannot hold the monopoly.[158]

In the following, we will discuss the dogmatic approach, the functional approach and the approach *sui generis*.

---

tot de rechtsvergelijking, Leuven, Universitaire Pers Leuven, 1998, 53; W. DEVROE, *Rechtsvergelijking in een context van europeanisering en globalisering*, Leuven, Acco, 2010, 50.

154 M. VAN HOECKE, "Deep Level Comparative Law" in M. VAN HOECKE (ed.), *Epistemology and Methodology of Comparative Law*, Oxford, Hart, 2004, 192.

155 D. PIETERS, "Functions of comparative law and practical methodology of comparing" in *Syllabus Research Master in Law*, Leuven-Tilburg, 2009, 18.

156 For an overview: M. SIEMS, *Comparative Law*, Cambridge, Cambridge University Press, 2014, 37–39; C. VALCKE and M. GRELLETTE, "Three Functions of Function in Comparative Legal Studies" in M. ADAMS and D. HEIRBAUT (eds.), *The Method and Culture of Comparative Law*, Oxford, Hart Publishing, 2014, 100–101.

157 J. HUSA, "Research Designs of Comparative Law" in M. ADAMS and D. HEIRBAUT (eds.), *The Method and Methodology*, 2014, 61.

158 J. HUSA, "Farewell to Functionalism of Methodological Tolerance?", *The Rabel Journal of Comparative and International Private Law* 2003, 422; R. MICHAELS, "The Functional Method of Comparative Law" in M. REIMANN and R. ZIMMERMANN (eds.), *The Oxford Handbook of Comparative Law*, Oxford, Oxford University Press, 2006, 341; G. SAMUEL, "Does One Need an Understanding of Methodology in Law Before One Can Understand Methodology in Comparative Law" in M. VAN HOECKE (ed.), *Methodologies of Legal Research*, Oxford, Hart Publishing, 2011, 181 and 186; J. DE CONINCK, "The Functional Method of Comparative Law: Quo Vadis?", *Rabels Zeitschrift für ausländisches und internationales Privatrecht* 2010, 321; E. ÖRÜCÜ, "Developing Comparative Law" in E. ÖRÜCÜ and D. NELKEN (eds.), *Comparative* Law, Oxford, Hart Publishing, 2007, 51; A.E. ODERKERK, *De preliminaire fase van het rechtsvergelijkend onderzoek*, Nijmegen, Ars Aequi Libri, 1999, 83; F. GORLÉ, G. BOURGEOIS, H. BOCKEN et al, *Rechtsvergelijking*, Mechelen, Kluwer, 2007, 33; M. ADAMS and D. HEIRBAUT, "Prolegomena to the Method and Culture of Comparative Law" in M. ADAMS ane D. HEIRBAUT (eds.), *The Method and Methodology of Comparative Law. Essays in Honour of Mark Van Hoecke,* Oxford, Hart Publishing, 2014, 6–7.

3.3.1.6.1 Dogmatic approach

When opting for a dogmatic approach, researchers will project a clearly-delineated legal concept or arrangement to a foreign legal system in order to detect "conceptually equivalent rules."[159] The dogmatic approach has proven to be useful for macro comparisons, comparisons between affiliated legal systems and first acquaintances with foreign legal systems.[160] Moreover, it can produce its results rather quickly.[161]

Legal scholars need to clarify and delineate the object of their comparison. In this respect, there are two options. First of all, it is possible to interpret the object according to the researchers' own national legal system. However, this gives the comparison a strong national perspective, which is largely criticized in legal doctrine[162], as it implies that a foreign legal system is approached throughout the concepts (and underlying structure) of another legal system.[163] Second, a researchers can put their own meaning to the object of comparison. For example: when the object of comparison is 'procedures of administrative courts', it will soon become clear that the concepts 'administrative law' and 'courts' can differ from one legal system to another.[164] A researcher can therefore decide to draft a working definition of 'court' considering e.g. the independence of the decision-making body, the expertise of the decision-making body, the possibility to apply for an appeal etc.[165]

A dogmatic approach holds several dangers.[166] First, homonymic concepts can have different meanings. PINTENS refers to the difference between the English *act* and the French *acte*, or the different meaning of *jurisprudence* in English (*legal doctrine*) and French (*case law*).[167] Also WATSON warns that the

---

159 Translation of: "begripsmatig equivalente rechtsregels" A.E. ODERKERK, *De preliminaire fase van het rechtsvergelijkend onderzoek*, Nijmegen, Ars Aequi Libri, 1999, 75; W. DEVROE, *Rechtsvergelijking in een context van europeanisering en globalisering*, Leuven, Acco, 2010, 38; F. GORLÉ, G. BOURGEOIS, H. BOCKEN et al, *Rechtsvergelijking*, Mechelen, Kluwer, 2007, 32; W. PINTENS, *Inleiding tot de rechtsvergelijking*, Leuven, Universitaire Pers Leuven, 1998, 84.

160 D. PIETERS, "Functions of comparative law and practical methodology of comparing" in *Syllabus Research Master in Law*, Leuven-Tilburg, 2009, 13; W. DEVROE, *Rechtsvergelijking in een context van europeanisering en globalisering*, Leuven, Acco, 2010, 39; A.E. ODERKERK, *De preliminaire fase van het rechtsvergelijkend onderzoek*, Nijmegen, Ars Aequi Libri, 1999, 83.

161 F. GORLÉ, G. BOURGEOIS, H. BOCKEN et al, *Rechtsvergelijking*, Mechelen, Kluwer, 2007, 32.

162 See: M. SIEMS, *Comparative Law*, Cambridge, Cambridge University Press, 2014, 16.

163 VALCKE demonstrates on the basis of her own research the danger of using concepts which are derived from one of the systems under comparison. C. VALCKE, "Reflections on comparative law methodology – getting inside contract law" in M. ADAMS and J. BOMHOFF (eds.), *Practice and Theory in Comparative Law*, Cambridge, Cambridge University Press, 2012, 30–32.

164 M. VAN HOECKE, "Deep Level Comparative Law" in M. VAN HOECKE (ed.), *Epistemology and Methodology of Comparative Law*, Oxford, Hart, 2004, 169.

165 M. VAN HOECKE, "Deep Level Comparative Law" in M. VAN HOECKE (ed.), *Epistemology and Methodology of Comparative Law*, Oxford, Hart, 2004, 169.

166 See also: M. VAN HOECKE, "Deep Level Comparative Law" in M. VAN HOECKE (ed.), *Epistemology and Methodology of Comparative Law*, Oxford, Hart, 2004, 175.

167 W. PINTENS, *Inleiding tot de rechtsvergelijking*, Leuven, Universitaire Pers Leuven, 1998, 52.

concepts *contrat, tribunal administratif, prescription* and *juge de paix* in French are not necessarily the same as *contract, administrative tribunal, prescription* and *justice of the peace* in English.[168]

Second, a comparative study departing from a national legal concept is likely to search for its foreign counterpart on the exact same place as where the concept is situated in the national legal system (same codex, same legal discipline, etc.).[169] If there is no trace of the concept in that specific part of the foreign legal system, researchers cannot simply conclude that the concept does not exist in that system. On the contrary, they also have to screen the other parts of the foreign legal system.[170]

Third, it is possible that a national legal concept does not as such occur in another legal system. After all, different legal systems can use different legal concepts or constructs. An example would be the concept *foundation* in Belgian law and the *trust* in common law traditions.[171] Although the concept of *foundation* does not exist in common law, the *trust* can fulfil the same objectives. This kind of nuance is rather difficult to spot when using a purely dogmatic approach, departing from a national-oriented concept.

Finally, the sources of a dogmatic approach are traditionally limited to formal legal sources, i.e. legislation in continental legal systems and hard cases in common law traditions.[172] Researchers should be aware of this limitation. After all, the content and scope of legal rules in formal law can be quite different from their application in practice.[173]

3.3.1.6.2 Functional approach

The functional approach to comparative law is based on the premise that "the legal system of every society faces essentially the same problems, and solves these problems by quite different means though often with similar results."[174] Based on this *praesumptio similitudinis* the functional approach does not depart from a fixed concept, but from a specific problem or a concrete situation[175], which can

168 A. WATSON, *Legal Transplants*, Edinburgh, Scottish Academic Press, 1974, 11.

169 K. ZWEIGERT and H. KÖTZ, *An Introduction to Comparative Law*, Oxford, Oxford University Press, 1997, 35.

170 See also: W. PINTENS, *Inleiding tot de rechtsvergelijking*, Leuven, Universitaire Pers Leuven, 1998, 89–90.

171 Example derived from F. GORLÉ, G. BOURGEOIS, H. BOCKEN et al, *Rechtsvergelijking*, Mechelen, Kluwer, 2007, 32–33.

172 F. GORLÉ, G. BOURGEOIS, H. BOCKEN et al, *Rechtsvergelijking*, Mechelen, Kluwer, 2007, 32.

173 W. DEVROE, *Rechtsvergelijking in een context van europeanisering en globalisering*, Leuven, Acco, 2010, 39.

174 K. ZWEIGERT and H. KÖTZ, *An Introduction to Comparative Law*, Oxford, Oxford University Press, 1997, 34.

175 A.E. ODERKERK, *De preliminaire fase van het rechtsvergelijkend onderzoek*, Nijmegen, Ars Aequi Libri, 1999, 67; D. PIETERS, "Functions of comparative law and practical methodology

be of a factual, legal, social or economic nature.[176] It is up to the comparative researchers to investigate how different legal systems deal with these similar problems or situations and which solution(s) they offer.[177] The functional approach is frequently used for micro comparisons.[178]

Because of the focus on a specific problem or situation, legal scholars have to take into account the broader legal context of the foreign system[179]: what is the structure of the legal system, what are the underlying fundamental principles and theories[180], what is the role of judges and administrative authorities, what about the relationship or interaction between legal provisions, legal institutions and legal disciplines[181], etc.? A comparison with a functional approach should also be interested in the social, political, economic, cultural, religious, demographic and/or geographic context of the foreign legal system.[182] Even the role of law in society and the way a society condemns violations of the law can be valuable information.[183]

---

of comparing" in *Syllabus Research Master in Law*, Leuven-Tilburg, 2009, 12; J. DE CONINCK, "The Functional Method of Comparative Law: Quo Vadis?", *Rabels Zeitschrift für ausländisches und internationales Privatrecht* 2010, 323.

176 A.E. ODERKERK, *De preliminaire fase van het rechtsvergelijkend onderzoek*, Nijmegen, Ars Aequi Libri, 1999, 70–71 (and references).

177 J. HUSA, "Research Designs of Comparative Law" in M. ADAMS and D. HEIRBAUT (eds.), *The Method and Methodology*, 2014, 60; W. DEVROE, *Rechtsvergelijking in een context van europeanisering en globalisering*, Leuven, Acco, 2010, 39; F. GORLÉ, G. BOURGEOIS, H. BOCKEN et al, *Rechtsvergelijking*, Mechelen, Kluwer, 2007, 32; D. PIETERS, "Functions of comparative law and practical methodology of comparing" in *Syllabus Research Master in Law*, Leuven-Tilburg, 2009, 24.

178 D. PIETERS, "Functions of comparative law and practical methodology of comparing" in *Syllabus Research Master in Law*, Leuven-Tilburg, 2009, 13; W. PINTENS, *Inleiding tot de rechtsvergelijking*, Leuven, Universitaire Pers Leuven, 1998, 64.

179 J. BELL, "Legal Research and the Distinctiveness of Comparative Law" in M. VAN HOECKE (ed.), *Methodologies of Legal Research*, Oxford, Hart Publishing, 2011, 170; W. DEVROE, *Rechtsvergelijking in een context van europeanisering en globalisering*, Leuven, Acco, 2010, 49; K. ZWEIGERT and H. KÖTZ, *An Introduction to Comparative Law*, Oxford, Oxford University Press, 1997, 36; M. VAN HOECKE, "Deep Level Comparative Law" in M. VAN HOECKE (ed.), *Epistemology and Methodology of Comparative Law*, Oxford, Hart, 2004, 167; M. SCHMITTHOFF, "The science of comparative law", *C.L.J.* 1939, 98; C. MORRIS and C. MURPHY, *Getting a PhD in Law*, Oxford, Hart Publishing, 2011, 37.

180 M. SIEMS, *Comparative Law*, Cambridge, Cambridge University Press, 2014, 19.

181 G. DANNEMANN, "Comparative Law: Study of Similarities or Differences?" in M. REIMANN and R. ZIMMERMANN (eds.), *The Oxford Handbook of Comparative Law*, Oxford, Oxford University Press, 2006, 413–414.

182 G. DANNEMANN, "Comparative Law: Study of Similarities or Differences?" in M. REIMANN and R. ZIMMERMANN (eds.), *The Oxford Handbook of Comparative Law*, Oxford, Oxford University Press, 2006, 404; M. SALTER and J. MASON, *Writing Law Dissertations*, Essex, Pearson, 2007, 183; M. SCHMITTHOFF, "The science of comparative law", *C.L.J.* 1939, 99; J. HUSA, "Comparative Law, Legal Linguistics and Methodology of Legal Doctrine" in M. VAN HOECKE (ed.), *Methodologies of Legal Research*, Oxford, Hart Publishing, 2011, 222; W. DEVROE, *Rechtsvergelijking in een context van europeanisering en globalisering*, Leuven, Acco, 2010, 50.

183 D. PIETERS, "Functions of comparative law and practical methodology of comparing" in *Syllabus Research Master in Law*, Leuven-Tilburg, 2009, 16–17.

When studying foreign legal systems with a functional approach, researchers cannot be led by concepts, principles and structures of their own legal system.[184] Even the mindset of their own system or society towards the problem or situation under comparison cannot play a part.[185] To avoid such ethnocentrism, legal scholars can use functional descriptions.[186] For example, instead of using the concept 'incapacity benefit', researchers can use a functional description: "income protection of those who cannot work (anymore) due to their state of health".[187] By using these kinds of functional descriptions legal scholars keep sufficient distance from the concepts and structures of their own legal system.[188]

Although ethnocentrism should be avoided as much as possible, it is impossible to compare in a completely objective or neutral way. Law – and therefore also foreign law – is always approached with one's own national legal tradition, society and preconceptions at the back of their mind.[189] FRANKENBERG therefore says:

> "instead of pretending to the posture of a neutral, objective, and disinterested observer, the comparatist has to regard herself as being involved: involved in an ongoing, particular social practice constituted and pervaded by law; involved in a given legal tradition (a peculiar story of law); and involved in a specific mode of thinking and talking about law."[190]

Only when legal scholars are aware of their personal perspective towards the foreign legal system, they can uncover what is exactly new or different about that system.[191]

---

184 K. ZWEIGERT and H. KÖTZ, *An Introduction to Comparative Law*, Oxford, Oxford University Press, 1997, 35; M. ADAMS, "Doing What Doesn't come Naturally. On the Distinctiveness of Comparative Law" in M. VAN HOECKE (ed.), *Methodologies of Legal Research*, Oxford, Hart Publishing, 2011, 234; J.C. REITZ, "How to Do Comparative Law?", *Am.J.Comp.L.* 1998, 621; D. PIETERS, "Functions of comparative law and practical methodology of comparing" in *Syllabus Research Master in Law*, Leuven-Tilburg, 2009, 23–24; F. GORLÉ, G. BOURGEOIS, H. BOCKEN et al, *Rechtsvergelijking*, Mechelen, Kluwer, 2007, 33.

185 J. HUSA, "Farewell to Functionalism of Methodological Tolerance?", *The Rabel Journal of Comparative and International Private Law* 2003, 423.

186 M. SIEMS, *Comparative Law*, Cambridge, Cambridge University Press, 2014, 14.

187 See also: D. PIETERS, *Sociale-zekerheidsrechtsvergelijking ten dienste van Europa*, Deventer, Kluwer, 1992, 36.

188 K. ZWEIGERT and H. KÖTZ, *An Introduction to Comparative Law*, Oxford, Oxford University Press, 1997, 34–35; W. PINTENS, *Inleiding tot de rechtsvergelijking*, Leuven, Universitaire Pers Leuven, 1998, 90.

189 G. FRANKENBERG, "Critical Comparisons: Re-thinking Comparative Law", *Harv.Intern'l L.J.* 1985, 443; W. DEVROE, *Rechtsvergelijking in een context van europeanisering en globalisering*, Leuven, Acco, 2010, 42.

190 G. FRANKENBERG, "Critical Comparisons: Re-thinking Comparative Law", *Harv.Int'l L.J.* 1985, 443. See also: J. DE CONINCK, "The Functional Method of Comparative Law: Quo Vadis?", *Rabels Zeitschrift für ausländisches und internationales Privatrecht* 2010, 328 and references.

191 G. FRANKENBERG, "Critical Comparisons: Re-thinking Comparative Law", *Harv.Int'l L.J.* 1985, 443.

To end with, the functional approach to comparative law is characterized by extensive source material: formal law, case law, legal doctrine, customs, alternative dispute resolutions, collective labour agreements, circulars, non-legal arrangements, etc.[192] After all, the functional approach departs from a specific problem or situation and tries to find out how other legal systems deal with them. Those systems can settle the problem in formal legislation, but can also deal with it in customary law, case law, non-legal mechanisms or even social stigmas.[193] ZWEIGERT and KÖTZ state that a functional comparison "should go as deep as possible into his chosen system".[194] However, it depends on the specific circumstances of the research how far the researcher *should* go (micro v macro), *can* go (time and page limits) and which *contexts* are relevant to the comparison (legal, social, political, economic, religious).[195]

3.3.1.6.3 Sui generis approach

Several variations to the traditional approaches (dogmatic and functional) exist. A first example is the typological approach searching for different solutions to the same problem in order to create a general typology under which related solutions can be ranged. A second example is the *case-oriented factual approach,* in which a specific problem is converted into a case.[196] Thirdly, there is also a *structural comparison,* which uncovers similar structures in different legal systems in order to find out their function in each system and how they have developed.[197] The two

---

192 K. ZWEIGERT and H. KÖTZ, *An Introduction to Comparative Law,* Oxford, Oxford University Press, 1997, 35; M. VAN HOECKE, "Deep Level Comparative Law" in M. VAN HOECKE (ed.), *Epistemology and Methodology of Comparative Law,* Oxford, Hart, 2004, 168; G. DANNEMANN, "Comparative Law: Study of Similarities or Differences?" in M. REIMANN and R. ZIMMERMANN (eds.), *The Oxford Handbook of Comparative Law,* Oxford, Oxford University Press, 2006, 408; J.C. REITZ, "How to Do Comparative Law?", *Am.J.Comp.L.* 1998, 628–630; W. DEVROE, *Rechtsvergelijking in een context van europeanisering en globalisering,* Leuven, Acco, 2010, 48.

193 R. MICHAELS, "The Functional Method of Comparative Law" in M. REIMANN and R. ZIMMERMANN (eds.), *The Oxford Handbook of Comparative Law,* Oxford, Oxford University Press, 2006, 364; J. HUSA, "Farewell to Functionalism of Methodological Tolerance?", *The Rabel Journal of Comparative and International Private Law* 2003, 423; K. ZWEIGERT and H. KÖTZ, *An Introduction to Comparative Law,* Oxford, Oxford University Press, 1997, 38; J.C. REITZ, "How to Do Comparative Law?", *Am.J.Comp.L.* 1998, 630; C. VALCKE and M. GRELLETTE, "Three Functions of Function in Comparative Legal Studies" in M. ADAMS and D. HEIRBAUT (eds.), *The Method and Culture of Comparative Law,* Oxford, Hart Publishing, 2014, 103–104.

194 K. ZWEIGERT and H. KÖTZ, *An Introduction to Comparative Law,* Oxford, Oxford University Press, 1997, 40.

195 M. VAN HOECKE, "Deep Level Comparative Law" in M. VAN HOECKE (ed.), *Epistemology and Methodology of Comparative Law,* Oxford, Hart, 2004, 167.

196 ODERKERK refers to SCHLESINGER; A.E. ODERKERK, *De preliminaire fase van het rechtsvergelijkend onderzoek,* Nijmegen, Ars Aequi Libri, 1999, 72 (and references).

197 J. HUSA, "Research Designs of Comparative Law – Methodology" in M. ADAMS and D. HEIRBAUT (eds.), *The Method and Methodology,* Oxford, Hart Publishing, 2014, 62.

final examples concern the *twofold comparison* and the *two-stage comparison*. The former compares legal systems in a twofold way: legal systems are first compared in a static way (on the basis of the current state of law) and afterwards in a dynamic way (on the basis of their evolution and developments through time).[198] The two-stage comparison involves a comparison in two stages: in a first stage, all selected legal systems are explored in a general way in order to select some of them to deal with more extensively in the second stage of the comparison.[199]

These examples show how legal scholars can compare with a *sui generis* approach, which is adapted to the specifics of their research. After all, the reasons for doing a comparison can be quite diverse and therefore each comparative study will have its own characteristics. This inevitably leads to a plurality of approaches.[200] It is therefore up to the comparative researchers to motivate and justify their *sui generis* approach.[201]

3.3.2 COMPARISON PROCESS

3.3.2.1 Describing legal systems

Every comparison starts with a description of the selected legal systems.[202] After all, without a prior description there is nothing to compare with.[203] Regardless of the chosen approach (dogmatic, functional, *sui generis)*, researchers have to

198 L. KESTEMONT, *Naar een rechtswetenschappelijke methodeleer. Een expliciet methodologisch kader voor rechtswetenschappelijk onderzoek in het socialezekerheidsrecht*, Bruges, die Keure (reeks Begasoz/ Abetrass), 2017, 139. Approach derived from J. VAN LANGENDONCK, *De harmonisering van de sociale verzekering voor gezondheidszorgen in de E.E.G.*, PhD KU Leuven, 1971.

199 L. KESTEMONT, *Naar een rechtswetenschappelijke methodeleer. Een expliciet methodologisch kader voor rechtswetenschappelijk onderzoek in het socialezekerheidsrecht*, Bruges, die Keure (reeks Begasoz/ Abetrass), 2017, 139. Approach derived from S.M.E. VANSTEENKISTE, *Sociale zekerheid, federalisme en de Europese gemeenschap. Een rechtsvergelijkende studie naar de verdeling van bevoegdheden inzake sociale zekerheid in samengestelde staten en in de Europese gemeenschap*, PhD University of Tilburg, 1995.

200 M. SIEMS, *Comparative Law*, Cambridge, Cambridge University Press, 2014, 33; M. ADAMS and D. HEIRBAUT, "Prolegomena to the Method and Culture of Comparative Law" in M. ADAMS and D. HEIRBAUT (eds.), *The Method and Methodology of Comparative Law. Essays in Honour of Mark Van Hoecke*, Oxford, Hart Publishing, 2014, 6–7.

201 H. TIJSSEN, *De juridische dissertatie onder de loep*, The Hague, Boom juridische uitgevers, 2009, 77.

202 K. ZWEIGERT and H. KÖTZ, *An Introduction to Comparative Law*, Oxford, Oxford University Press, 1997, 6 and 43; M. SCHMITTHOFF, "The science of comparative law", *C.L.J.* 1939, 95; R.A.J. VAN GESTEL and J.B.M. VRANKEN, "Rechtswetenschappelijke artikelen", *NJB* 2007, 1454; M. ADAMS, "Doing What Doesn't Come Naturally. On the Distinctiveness of Comparative Law" in M. VAN HOECKE (ed.), *Methodologies of Legal Research*, Oxford, Hart Publishing, 2011, 233; M. ADAMS, "Wat de rechtsvergelijking vermag", *AA* 2011, 195; F. GORLÉ, G. BOURGEOIS, H. BOCKEN et al., *Rechtsvergelijking*, Mechelen, Kluwer, 2007, 64.

203 J.C. REITZ, "How to Do Comparative Law?", *Am.J.Comp.L.* 1998, 619.

describe in a precise and objective manner: "*sine ira et studio*".[204] Moreover – and as previously mentioned – the description of legal systems has to be balanced, implying that all legal systems are dealt with in the same way.[205] A more extensive description of one legal system can hinder its comparability with the other.[206]

Legal scholars tend to use a fixed structure when describing legal systems, as it facilitates their comparison later on. Using such predetermined outline avoids that researchers look at foreign legal systems without any structural direction or protection against an overload of information. In addition, a fixed structure will immediately indicate several interesting leads for comparison: modalities, formalities, conditions, exceptions, etc. The outline of the description of legal systems will therefore be directive for their comparison later on. However, legal scholars should use *fixed description outlines* in a conscious and moderate way, for it is possible that the structure proposed does not (entirely) fit the systematics and coherence of a foreign legal system. In that case, the fixed description outline could suffocate the uniqueness of a particular system. It is therefore up to the legal scholar to try and develop a description outline that can indicate interesting leads for comparison, without harming the particularities of the legal systems involved.

With respect to the description of foreign legal systems, there are three points of interest regarding language. First of all, researchers should master both the standard and legal language of the legal systems under comparison.[207] Moreover, they have to be careful with false legal synonyms[208] or legal homonyms.[209] Dictionaries can be useful, but also here some prudence is necessary: general dictionaries do not contain that much information on legal jargon and even 'legal' dictionaries often only present a brief clarification, regardless of a specific context.[210] Ideally, legal scholars look up foreign legal concepts in authoritative national handbooks or encyclopaedia.[211]

---

204 M. SCHMITTHOFF, "The science of comparative law", *C.L.J.* 1939, 99; K. ZWEIGERT and H. KÖTZ, *An Introduction to Comparative Law*, Oxford, Oxford University Press, 1997, 43.

205 C. MORRIS and C. MURPHY, *Getting a PhD in Law*, Oxford, Hart Publishing, 2011, 37.

206 J.B.M. VRANKEN, "Algemeen Deel. Een synthese" in *Mr. C. Assers Handleiding tot de beoefening van het Nederlands Burgerlijk Recht*, Deventer, Kluwer, 2014, 19.

207 F. GORLÉ, G. BOURGEOIS, H. BOCKEN et al., *Rechtsvergelijking*, Mechelen, Kluwer, 2007, 32; W. DEVROE, *Rechtsvergelijking in een context van europeanisering en globalisering*, Leuven, Acco, 2010, 51.

208 These are "concepts which refer to equal or similar legal constructs, but with different legal modalities, consequences, etc." W. DEVROE, Rechtsvergelijking in een context van europeanisering en globalisering, Leuven, Acco, 2010, 51.

209 These are concepts with the same or a rather similar spelling/pronounciation, but with a different legal meaning: W. PINTENS, *Inleiding tot de rechtsvergelijking*, Leuven, Universitaire Pers Leuven, 1998, 52; F. GORLÉ, G. BOURGEOIS, H. BOCKEN et al, *Rechtsvergelijking*, Mechelen, Kluwer, 2007, 58; W. DEVROE, *Rechtsvergelijking in een context van europeanisering en globalisering*, Leuven, Acco, 2010, 51; A. WATSON, *Legal Transplants*, Edinburgh, Scottish Academic Press, 1974, 11.

210 W. DEVROE, *Rechtsvergelijking in een context van europeanisering en globalisering*, Leuven, Acco, 2010, 52.

211 F. GORLÉ, G. BOURGEOIS, H. BOCKEN et al, *Rechtsvergelijking*, Mechelen, Kluwer, 2007, 60.

Second, when describing legal systems legal scholars can ask help from local experts. Reasons to involve such experts are diverse: legal scholars do not (sufficiently) master the language of a foreign legal system, they want to verify their description or they want to complete their description with insights from the *law in action*.[212] In these cases, assistance of national experts – through informal meetings, interviews, questionnaires, etc. – can be very useful.

Third, describing a foreign legal system implies a translation: foreign legal jargon is translated into the jargon of the writing language.[213] However, there is discussion on the desirability of such translations. Some authors think that a translation is necessary in order to make foreign concepts understandable to the reader, whereas others support to keep the original concepts so that the reader cannot be misled when it comes to the exact meaning of the concepts.[214] This discussion specifically comes up when a foreign legal concept does not have an (exact) equivalent in the researcher's writing language.[215] In this situation, DE GROOT lists four possible approaches.[216] First of all, the researcher can use a concept that has nearly the same meaning as the foreign concept. This is only an option when both concepts match in their essence. Second, a researcher can decide to use the original foreign concept and not make a translation.[217] In this case, a brief clarification of the concept is of course necessary. Third, instead of using a foreign concept the researcher may opt to use a brief description: the elements included in the description allow the reader – who is familiar with the writing language – to understand the foreign legal concept. The use of these kinds of brief descriptions depends on their length and complexity. Finally, a researcher could look for a neology. The meaning of the new word should be understandable to readers who are familiar with the writing language. It is always a good idea to find out whether other authors already proposed a neology for the foreign concept under consideration.

When describing foreign legal systems, researchers should stick to their particularities: existing hierarchy between legal norms, prevailing

---

212 L. KESTEMONT, *Naar een rechtswetenschappelijke methodeleer. Een expliciet methodologisch kader voor rechtswetenschappelijk onderzoek in het socialezekerheidsrecht*, Bruges, die Keure (series Begasoz/ Abetrass), 2017, 197.

213 G.-R. DE GROOT, "Legal Translation" in J.M. SMITS (ed.), *Elgar Encyclopedia of Comparative Law*, Cheltenham, Edward Elgar, 2006, 423.

214 M. SIEMS, *Comparative Law*, Cambridge, Cambridge University Press, 2014, 17.

215 G.-R. DE GROOT, "Legal Translation" in J.M. SMITS (ed.), *Elgar Encyclopedia of Comparative Law*, Cheltenham, Edward Elgar, 2006, 424; W. DEVROE, *Rechtsvergelijking in een context van europeanisering en globalisering*, Leuven, Acco, 2010, 52.

216 For more information and references to other authors, see: G.-R. DE GROOT, "Legal Translation" in J.M. SMITS (ed.), *Elgar Encyclopedia of Comparative Law*, Cheltenham, Edward Elgar, 2006, 424–429.

217 See also: W. DEVROE, *Rechtsvergelijking in een context van europeanisering en globalisering*, Leuven, Acco, 2010, 53; F. GORLÉ, G. BOURGEOIS, H. BOCKEN et al, *Rechtsvergelijking*, Mechelen, Kluwer, 2007, 61.

interpretations of legal rules, internal structure and cohesion, etc.[218] This way the description of the foreign legal system will correspond to the descriptions made by the own legal community.[219]

3.3.2.2 Comparing legal systems

Comparative law is not simply describing different legal systems.[220] A parallel reproduction (*juxtaposing*) is insufficient.[221] There needs to be an explicit comparison that confronts the different legal systems with each other in order to uncover similarities and differences.[222] After all, it is up to the researchers to list similarities and differences in order to avoid that readers might draw wrong conclusions from the descriptions.[223]

The reason(s) for comparison will determine whether a researcher pays more attention to similarities or to differences.[224] A legal scholar who looks into harmonization measures will focus on common principles of different Member States[225], whereas a research wanting to figure out the most tax-friendly legal

---

218 D. PIETERS, "Functions of comparative law and practical methodology of comparing" in *Syllabus Research Master in Law*, Leuven-Tilburg, 2009, 16; W. DEVROE, *Rechtsvergelijking in een context van europeanisering en globalisering*, Leuven, Acco, 2010, 48–49; F. GORLÉ, G. BOURGEOIS, H. BOCKEN et al, *Rechtsvergelijking*, Mechelen, Kluwer, 2007, 40.

219 S. VOGENAUER, "Sources of Law and Legal Method in Comparative Law" in M. REIMANN and R. ZIMMERMANN (eds.), *The Oxford Handbook of Comparative Law*, Oxford, Oxford University Press, 2006, 872.

220 D. PIETERS, "Functions of comparative law and practical methodology of comparing" in *Syllabus Research Master in Law*, Leuven-Tilburg, 2009, 1, 3–4.

221 W. DEVROE, *Rechtsvergelijking in een context van europeanisering en globalisering*, Leuven, Acco, 2010, 53; M. VAN HOECKE, "Deep Level Comparative Law" in M. VAN HOECKE (ed.), *Epistemology and Methodology of Comparative Law*, Oxford, Hart, 2004, 166; K. ZWEIGERT and H. KÖTZ, *An Introduction to Comparative Law*, Oxford, Oxford University Press, 1997, 4 and 43; J.C. REITZ, "How to Do Comparative Law?", *Am.J.Comp.L.* 1998, 618; F.F. STONE, "The end to be served by comparative law", *Tul.L.Rev.* 1950–51, 327; M.M. SIEMS, "Legal Originality", *O.J.L.S.* 2008, 151; F. GORLÉ, G. BOURGEOIS, H. BOCKEN et al, *Rechtsvergelijking*, Mechelen, Kluwer, 2007, 64.

222 M. ADAMS, "Wat de rechtsvergelijking vermag", *AA* 2011, 198; W. PINTENS, *Inleiding tot de rechtsvergelijking*, Leuven, Universitaire Pers Leuven, 1998, 16; J.C. REITZ, "How to Do Comparative Law?", *Am.J.Comp.L.* 1998, 620; W. DEVROE, *Rechtsvergelijking in een context van europeanisering en globalisering*, Leuven, Acco, 2010, 53; M. SIEMS, *Comparative Law*, Cambridge, Cambridge University Press, 2014, 20; K. LEMMENS, "Comparative law as an act of modesty: a pragmatic and realistic approach to comparative legal scholarship" in M. ADAMS and J. BOMHOFF (eds.), *Practice and Theory in Comparative Law*, Cambridge, Cambridge University Press, 2012, 322.

223 J.C. REITZ, "How to Do Comparative Law?", *Am.J.Comp.L.* 1998, 619.

224 G. DANNEMANN, "Comparative Law: Study of Similarities or Differences?" in M. REIMANN and R. ZIMMERMANN (eds.), *The Oxford Handbook of Comparative Law*, Oxford, Oxford University Press, 2006, 415; M.W. HESSELINK, *Contractenrecht in perspectief*, The Hague, Boom Juridische uitgevers, 2004, 202.

225 J. HILL, "Comparative Law, Law Reform and Legal Theory", *O.J.L.S.* 1989, 110; G. DANNEMANN, "Comparative Law: Study of Similarities or Differences?" in M. REIMANN

system is going to concentrate on main differences.[226] However, despite the focus of every comparison, it is important to map both similarities and differences.[227] Only the combination allows to fully grasp the systems under comparison.[228]

Legal systems can be compared in different ways. First of all, they can be first described individually and compared afterwards. In the comparative part legal scholars can use a "parallel column".[229] Such column allows to list the rules/particularities/solutions of the studied legal systems in a way that the reader can immediately grasp the similarities and differences. Second, it is possible to split the subject matter into different parts and to discuss each part for all the legal systems at once.[230] This way the similarities and differences of each part are discussed immediately. This kind of "explicit comparison"[231] is interesting, but is not that obvious for technical legal matters: dividing a subject matter into different parts can give a fragmented impression and can cause some confusion.

In the end, it is up to the researcher to decide. VALCKE summarizes the advantages and disadvantages as follows:

> "As the first pattern involves diving in and out of the system only once (when describing the particular system), it serves to emphasize the internal coherence of each system, possibly at risk of downplaying its various points of connection with the other system, whereas the movement of constant back and forth between the systems under the second pattern suggests that it conversely serves to underscore the connections between the systems, perhaps to the detriment of their internal coherence as separate systems."[232]

---

and R. ZIMMERMANN (eds.), *The Oxford Handbook of Comparative Law*, Oxford, Oxford University Press, 2006, 415.

226 G. DANNEMANN, "Comparative Law: Study of Similarities or Differences?" in M. REIMANN and R. ZIMMERMANN (eds.), *The Oxford Handbook of Comparative Law*, Oxford, Oxford University Press, 2006, 415 (see also: 404–405).

227 J. BELL, "Legal Research and the Distinctiveness of Comparative Law" in M. VAN HOECKE (ed.), *Methodologies of Legal Research*, Oxford, Hart Publishing, 2011, 174; E. ÖRÜCÜ, "Developing Comparative Law" in E. ÖRÜCÜ and D. NELKEN (eds.), *Comparative* Law, Oxford, Hart Publishing, 2007, 50.

228 G. DANNEMANN, "Comparative Law: Study of Similarities or Differences?" in M. REIMANN and R. ZIMMERMANN (eds.), *The Oxford Handbook of Comparative Law*, Oxford, Oxford University Press, 2006, 399 and 419.

229 F.F. STONE, "The end to be served by comparative law", *Tul.L.Rev.* 1950–51, 326. See also: C. VALCKE, "Reflections on comparative law methodology – getting inside contract law" in M. ADAMS and J. BOMHOFF (eds.), *Practice and Theory in Comparative Law*, Cambridge, Cambridge University Press, 2012, 44.

230 See also: C. VALCKE, "Reflections on comparative law methodology – getting inside contract law" in M. ADAMS and J. BOMHOFF (eds.), *Practice and Theory in Comparative Law*, Cambridge, Cambridge University Press, 2012, 44.

231 J.C. REITZ, "How to Do Comparative Law?", *Am.J.Comp.L.* 1998, 634.

232 C. VALCKE, "Reflections on comparative law methodology – getting inside contract law" in M. ADAMS and J. BOMHOFF (eds.), *Practice and Theory in Comparative Law*, Cambridge, Cambridge University Press, 2012, 44.

Finally, as the comparison will indicate which features legal systems have in common and which not, legal scholars may decide to categorize the studied systems.[233] At that moment, it is up to the researcher to decide which criteria will be 'decisive' for the classification of the legal systems.[234]

3.3.2.3 Explaining uncovered differences and similarities

Legal scholars will try to explain the uncovered similarities and differences, as they can only be fully understood once they have been clarified in light of their own specific context.[235] The question is not 'what are the differences and similarities?', but '*why* do these differences and similarities exist?'[236] The answer to that question will never be easy, as legal systems may differ due to their legal, political, social, economic, geographical, cultural and historical background or tradition.[237] An excellent example is legislation on social security: the

---

233 C. VALCKE, "Reflections on comparative law methodology – getting inside contract law" in M. ADAMS and J. BOMHOFF (eds.), *Practice and Theory in Comparative Law*, Cambridge, Cambridge University Press, 2012, 45.

234 W. PINTENS, *Inleiding tot de rechtsvergelijking*, Leuven, Universitaire Pers Leuven, 1998, 86. G. SAMUEL, *Epistemology and Method in Law*, Aldershot, Ashgate, 2003, 219; N. JANSEN, "Comparative Law and Comparative Knowledge" in M. REIMANN and R. ZIMMERMANN (eds.), *The Oxford Handbook of Comparative Law*, Oxford, Oxford University Press, 2006, 317; C. VALCKE, "Reflections on comparative law methodology – getting inside contract law" in M. ADAMS and J. BOMHOFF (eds.), *Practice and Theory in Comparative Law*, Cambridge, Cambridge University Press, 2012, 45.

235 M. ADAMS, "Wat de rechtsvergelijking vermag", *AA* 2011, 198; W. DEVROE, *Rechtsvergelijking in een context van europeanisering en globalisering*, Leuven, Acco, 2010, 53; M. VAN HOECKE, *Is de rechtswetenschap een empirische wetenschap?*, The Hague, Boom Juridische uitgevers, 2010, 14. This search for explanations is also mentioned in: G. DANNEMANN, "Comparative Law: Study of Similarities or Differences?" in M. REIMANN and R. ZIMMERMANN (eds.), *The Oxford Handbook of Comparative Law*, Oxford, Oxford University Press, 2006, 416; J.C. REITZ, "How to Do Comparative Law?", *Am.J.Comp.L.* 1998, 626; D. PIETERS, "Reflections on the methodology of social security law comparison" in B. GREVE and D. PIETERS (eds.), *Social security in an interdisciplinary perspective*, Antwerp, Maklu, 1999, 104; J. HUSA, "Research Designs of Comparative Law – Methodology or Heuristics" in M. ADAMS and D. HEIRBAUT (eds.), *The Method and Culture of Comparative Law*, Oxford, Hart Publishing, 2014, 54.

236 D. PIETERS, "Functions of comparative law and practical methodology of comparing" in *Syllabus Research Master in Law*, Leuven-Tilburg, 2009, 14; R. VAN GESTEL and H.-W. MICKLITZ, "Revitalising Doctrinal Legal Research in Europe: What About Methodology?" in U. NEERGAARD, R. NIELSEN and L. ROSEBERRY (eds.), *European Legal Method – Paradoxes and Revitalisation*, Kopenhagen, DJØF Publishing, 2011, 58; K. LEMMENS, "Comparative law as an act of modesty: a pragmatic and realistic approach to comparative legal scholarship" in M. ADAMS and J. BOMHOFF (eds.), *Practice and Theory in Comparative Law*, Cambridge, Cambridge University Press, 2012, 322.

237 K. ZWEIGERT and H. KÖTZ, *An Introduction to Comparative Law*, Oxford, Oxford University Press, 1997, 44; J.C. REITZ, "How to Do Comparative Law?", *Am.J.Comp.L.* 1998, 627; F. GORLÉ, G. BOURGEOIS, H. BOCKEN et al, *Rechtsvergelijking*, Mechelen, Kluwer, 2007, 67; J. HUSA, "Comparative Law, Legal Linguistics and Methodology of Legal Doctrine" in M. VAN HOECKE (ed.), *Methodologies of Legal Research*, Oxford, Hart Publishing, 2011, 224; W. PINTENS, *Inleiding tot de rechtsvergelijking*, Leuven, Universitaire Pers Leuven,

organization and functioning of a social security system is based on a political/ society's vision on solidarity, insurance, individual responsibility, redistribution of wealth, social assistance etc.[238]

When legal scholars want to look for an explanation outside the legal system, e.g. historical, religious, cultural, political, economic and/or demographic factors[239], the research will adopt a multi- or interdisciplinary approach.[240] In this case, the researchers have to be sufficiently trained on how to gather/deal with non-legal knowledge, so that the explanation does not become a subjective mishmash of information gathered from different academic disciplines.[241]

3.3.2.4 *Evaluating results of comparison*

After describing, comparing and explaining, legal scholars will evaluate the results of their comparison.[242] The content of the evaluation depends on the original reason(s) for the comparison.[243] For example: researchers in search for inspiration in order to solve a national legal problem will evaluate the results in view of their own national system: which mechanisms from the foreign legal systems address the national legal problem, which foreign solutions fit the national legal system? Etc.

When pursuing the evaluation, researchers should take into account the limitations of their comparison.[244] Choices made with respect to the selected systems, consulted sources and approach for comparison may not be neglected.

1998, 90; W. DEVROE, *Rechtsvergelijking in een context van europeanisering en globalisering*, Leuven, Acco, 2010, 53.

238 M. VAN HOECKE, "Deep Level Comparative Law" in M. VAN HOECKE (ed.), *Epistemology and Methodology of Comparative Law*, Oxford, Hart, 2004, 191; W. PINTENS, *Inleiding tot de rechtsvergelijking*, Leuven, Universitaire Pers Leuven, 1998, 90.

239 W. DEVROE, *Rechtsvergelijking in een context van europeanisering en globalisering*, Leuven, Acco, 2010, 53; F. GORLÉ, G. BOURGEOIS, H. BOCKEN et al, *Rechtsvergelijking*, Mechelen, Kluwer, 2007, 33; J.C. REITZ, "How to Do Comparative Law?", *Am.J.Comp.L.* 1998, 627; D. PIETERS, "Functions of comparative law and practical methodology of comparing" in *Syllabus Research Master in Law*, Leuven-Tilburg, 2009, 14; M. SIEMS, *Comparative Law*, Cambridge, Cambridge University Press, 2014, 21.

240 K. ZWEIGERT and H. KÖTZ, *An Introduction to Comparative Law*, Oxford, Oxford University Press, 1997, 44; J.C. REITZ, "How to Do Comparative Law?", *Am.J.Comp.L.* 1998, 627; W. DEVROE, *Rechtsvergelijking in een context van europeanisering en globalisering*, Leuven, Acco, 2010, 54.

241 K. LEMMENS, "Comparative law as an act of modesty: a pragmatic and realistic approach to comparative legal scholarship" in M. ADAMS and J. BOMHOFF (eds.), *Practice and Theory in Comparative Law*, Cambridge, Cambridge University Press, 2012, 323.

242 K. ZWEIGERT and H. KÖTZ, *An Introduction to Comparative Law*, Oxford, Oxford University Press, 1997, 46; W. PINTENS, *Inleiding tot de rechtsvergelijking*, Leuven, Universitaire Pers Leuven, 1998, 91.

243 F. GORLÉ, G. BOURGEOIS, H. BOCKEN et al, *Rechtsvergelijking*, Mechelen, Kluwer, 2007, 69.

244 D. PIETERS, "Functions of comparative law and practical methodology of comparing" in *Syllabus Research Master in Law*, Leuven-Tilburg, 2009, 23.

3.4 METHODOLOGICAL FEATURES OF A THEORY-BUILDING RESEARCH OBJECTIVE

A theory-building research objective aims to abstract the essence from particular legal constructs in order to develop a model or a legal theory. In this section we discuss different types of theories, their general requirements, the premises of a theory, the practice of abstraction, the importance of concepts and classifications, and finally we draw attention to the need for dissent.

3.4.1 DIFFERENT TYPES OF THEORIES

Legal theories can relate to different aspects of a legal system.[245] DREIER uses the following distinction. First of all, there are *interpretative theories*. These theories focus on the meaning of legal rules and are therefore very concrete.[246]

Second, there are theories on the structure of a legal system.[247] They clarify underlying common features, subdivisions of legal institutions and their place within the broader legal system.[248] These theories contribute to a better understanding of the legal order and have an important "*lückenfüllende*" (gap-filling) function.[249] They are strongly linked with classification.

Third, there are *"Institutstheorien"*. Such theories focus on legal institutions and more specifically on the norms that regulate typical social relationships, such as sale, marriage, property, mortgage, etc.[250]

Fourth, a *"Prinzipientheorie"* concentrates on the content, legal nature and function of abstract norms, such as general legal norms or principles of law. These norms and principles can be determined in legislation, or can be implicit in case law or multiple regulations.[251]

Finally, there are also *"Grundbegriffstheorien"*, which look into basic concepts included in particular legal norms on subjective rights, legal bodies, debts, etc.[252]

---

245 A. PECZENIK refers to DREIER in "Scientia Juris. Legal Doctrine as knowledge of Law and as a Source of Law" in E. PATTARO (ed.), *A Treatise of Legal Philosophy and General Jurisprudence*, Dordrecht, Springer, 2005, 32.

246 R. DREIER, *Recht – Moral – Ideologie*, Frankfurt am Main, Suhrkamp, 1981, 73.

247 R. DREIER, *Recht – Moral – Ideologie*, Frankfurt am Main, Suhrkamp, 1981, 74.

248 R. DREIER, *Recht – Moral – Ideologie*, Frankfurt am Main, Suhrkamp, 1981, 75.

249 R. DREIER, *Recht – Moral – Ideologie*, Frankfurt am Main, Suhrkamp, 1981, 75–76.

250 R. DREIER, *Recht – Moral – Ideologie*, Frankfurt am Main, Suhrkamp, 1981, 75.

251 R. DREIER, *Recht – Moral – Ideologie*, Frankfurt am Main, Suhrkamp, 1981, 76.

252 R. DREIER, *Recht – Moral – Ideologie*, Frankfurt am Main, Suhrkamp, 1981, 77.

3.4.2 GENERAL REQUIREMENTS OF A LEGAL THEORY

All legal theories should meet the following requirements.[253] Firstly, a theory has to make current law more comprehensible. In this respect, it should cover the law as much as possible without contradicting it.[254] A change of positive law can therefore have an important effect on existing theories.[255] For example, new legal or societal circumstances may question an established theory or may lead to an alteration or even a new theory.[256] This new theory will try to eliminate the adverse or undesired consequences of the old one:

> "The legal doctrine on third party liability was developed as a reaction to the practices of large companies, such as breweries, inciting distributors of similar products or services, such as inns, who had an exclusive contract with a competing firm, to breach their contract. The doctrine of non-enforceability to third parties did not allow to act against these practices."[257]

Secondly, a theory has to be a closed and logical entity[258], implying consistency and absence of internal contradictions.[259] A theory should also be accurate. This means that both its scope of application and its modalities are clearly

---

253 See several authors refering to VON JHERING: P. SCHOLTEN, "Algemeen Deel" in *Asser's Handleiding tot de beoefening van het Nederlandsch Burgerlijk Recht*, Zwolle, W.E.J. Tjeenk Willink, 1954, 65–67 72–73; P.W. KAMPHUISEN, *Beschouwingen over rechtswetenschap*, Nijmegen, Dekker & Van De Vegt, 1938, 80; J.J.H. BRUGGINK, *Wat zegt Scholten over recht*, Zwolle, W.E.J. Tjeenk Willink, 1983, 169.

254 P.W. KAMPHUISEN, *Beschouwingen over rechtswetenschap*, Nijmegen, Dekker & Van De Vegt, 1938, 81.

255 J.J.H. BRUGGINK, *Wat zegt Scholten over recht*, Zwolle, W.E.J. Tjeenk Willink, 1983, 169; P. SCHOLTEN, "Algemeen Deel" in *Asser's Handleiding tot de beoefening van het Nederlandsch Burgerlijk Recht*, Zwolle, W.E.J. Tjeenk Willink, 1954, 65; P.W. KAMPHUISEN, *Beschouwingen over rechtswetenschap*, Nijmegen, Dekker & Van De Vegt, 1938, 81.

256 M. VAN HOECKE, *Is de rechtswetenschap een empirische wetenschap?*, The Hague, Boom Juridische uitgevers, 2010, 29; P. SCHOLTEN, "Algemeen Deel" in *Asser's Handleiding tot de beoefening van het Nederlandsch Burgerlijk Recht*, Zwolle, W.E.J. Tjeenk Willink, 1954, 65; J.J.H. BRUGGINK, *Wat zegt Scholten over recht*, Zwolle, W.E.J. Tjeenk Willink, 1983, 169; P.W. KAMPHUISEN, *Beschouwingen over rechtswetenschap*, Nijmegen, Dekker & Van De Vegt, 1938, 81.

257 Translation of: "Zo werd de leer van de 'derde-medeplichtigheid aan contractbreuk' uitgewerkt als reactie op praktijken van grote bedrijven, bijvoorbeeld brouwerijen, die verdelers van gelijkaardige producten of diensten, bijvoorbeeld herbergen die contractueel verbonden waren door een exclusiviteitscontract met een concurrerend bedrijf, aanzetten om contractbreuk te plegen. De algemene leer van de niet-tegenstelbaarheid van contracten aan derden liet niet toe hiertegen op te treden." M. VAN HOECKE, *Is de rechtswetenschap een empirische wetenschap?*, The Hague, Boom Juridische uitgevers, 2010, 31.

258 P. SCHOLTEN, "Algemeen Deel" in *Asser's Handleiding tot de beoefening van het Nederlandsch Burgerlijk Recht*, Zwolle, W.E.J. Tjeenk Willink, 1954, 66; J.J.H. BRUGGINK, *Wat zegt Scholten over recht*, Zwolle, W.E.J. Tjeenk Willink, 1983, 170.

259 M. VAN HOECKE, *Is de rechtswetenschap een empirische wetenschap?*, The Hague, Boom Juridische uitgevers, 2010, 26.

determined.[260] In this respect, border cases will play an important role.[261] Finally, each theory should be characterized by its simplicity and clarity and its conceptual framework should be as small as possible.[262]

3.4.3 PREMISES OF A LEGAL THEORY

Each theory is based on general assumptions or premises. Examples are: "the acceptance of the priority of European law over domestic law, or the acceptance of 'unwritten general principles of law' as a valid source of law".[263] Both examples are of an internal nature, i.e. derived from the legal system itself. However, legal scholars can also rely on external premises, i.e. derived from outside the legal system, such as prevailing assumptions or models in economics. In sum, the premises of a legal theory can be both of internal or of external nature. In the latter case, the research will become multi- or interdisciplinary.

The premises of a legal theory will serve as a framework during the process of developing the theory.[264] It is therefore of utmost importance to make them explicit.

3.4.4 ABSTRACTING THE ESSENCE

Theory-building is characterized by abstracting the essence from legal rules or cases. Such abstraction allows to see order and unity.[265] Concepts will play an important role, as they are "a translation of classifications in real life which are considered to be more relevant than other ones."[266] In this respect, they allow

---

260 M. VAN HOECKE, *Is de rechtswetenschap een empirische wetenschap?*, The Hague, Boom Juridische uitgevers, 2010, 28.

261 M. VAN HOECKE, *Is de rechtswetenschap een empirische wetenschap?*, The Hague, Boom Juridische uitgevers, 2010, 27.

262 P. SCHOLTEN, "Algemeen Deel" in *Asser's Handleiding tot de beoefening van het Nederlandsch Burgerlijk Recht*, Zwolle, W.E.J. Tjeenk Willink, 1954, 66–67; J.J.H. BRUGGINK, *Wat zegt Scholten over recht*, Zwolle, W.E.J. Tjeenk Willink, 1983, 170; P.W. KAMPHUISEN, *Beschouwingen over rechtswetenschap*, Nijmegen, Dekker & Van De Vegt, 1938, 56.

263 M. VAN HOECKE, "Legal Doctrine: Which Method(s) for What Kind of Discipline?" in M. VAN HOECKE (ed.), *Methodologies of Legal Research*, Oxford, Hart Publishing, 2011, 15.

264 M. VAN HOECKE, *Is de rechtswetenschap een empirische wetenschap?*, The Hague, Boom Juridische uitgevers, 2010, 24.

265 P.G. KORREL and O.W.M. KAMSTRA, *Sociaal wetenschappelijke & juridische methodologie*, Amsterdam, Melkman, 1991, 46–47.

266 Translation of: "vormen een vertaling van indelingen in de werkelijkheid die relevanter worden geacht dan andere indelingen") M. VAN HOECKE, *Is de rechtswetenschap een empirische wetenschap?*, The Hague, Boom Juridische uitgevers, 2010, 25.

to grasp, describe and order reality.[267] Classifications are therefore essential to theory-building.[268] If legal scholars, for example, wish to develop different models for the organization of disability schemes, they first have to gather and classify the different types of disability schemes.[269]

The above shows that when pursuing a theory-building research objective legal scholars will use concepts and classifications.[270] It is important to clarify their content and scope[271], as the exact meaning of legal concepts depends on the particular context and period in time.[272] Moreover, the scope of the concepts should be sufficiently clear, as the use of precise concepts will be beneficial to the theory.[273]

3.4.5 ATTENTION FOR DISSENT

Legal scholars cannot only refer to those authors – and their argumentation – who support the developed theory. After all, underpinning a theory may "not be confused with making a subjective plea for a personal preference."[274] Also authors with other viewpoints and different opinions should be addressed.[275] Moreover, it allows the creators of a theory to indicate their spot within the ongoing academic debate.[276]

---

267 M. VAN HOECKE, *Is de rechtswetenschap een empirische wetenschap?*, The Hague, Boom Juridische uitgevers, 2010, 24.

268 M. VAN HOECKE, *Is de rechtswetenschap een empirische wetenschap?*, The Hague, Boom Juridische uitgevers, 2010, 24–26.

269 Example from the meta-study of 45 PhDs on social security law: A.F. ROMMELSE, *De arbeidsongeschiktheidsverzekering: tussen publiek en privaat. Een beschrijving, analyse en waardering van de belangrijkste wijzigingen in het Nederlandse arbeidsongeschiktheidsstelsel tussen 1980 en 2010*, 2014, PhD University of Leiden.

270 J.M. BARENDRECHT, "Rechtswetenschap: stoffig of inventief?", *NJB* 1996, 712.

271 M. BARENDRECHT, J. VRANKEN, I. GIESEN, M.J. BORGERS, W. VAN DER BURG, H.E.B. TIJSSEN, G.C.G.J. VAN ROERMUND and W.H. VAN BOOM, "Methoden van rechtswetenschap: komen we verder?", *NJB* 2004, 1425.

272 With respect to 'open norms', see P.A. FRUYTIER, "Enkele beschouwingen over de interdisciplinaire rechtswetenschap. Braudel als uitgangspunt van een afbakening?", *AA* 2007, 834.

273 M. BARENDRECHT, J. VRANKEN, I. GIESEN, M.J. BORGERS, W. VAN DER BURG, H.E.B. TIJSSEN, G.C.G.J. VAN ROERMUND and W.H. VAN BOOM, "Methoden van rechtswetenschap: komen we verder?", *NJB* 2004, 1425.

274 Translation of: "niet verwarren met een subjectief pleidooi voor een eigen praktische voorkeur." N. HOEKX, K. VANHOVE en A. VERBEKE, "Yes we care! Bedenkingen over de (methode der) rechtswetenschap", *RW* 2008–09, 1786.

275 C.J.J.M. STOLKER, "Wat maakt een juridisch tijdschrift wetenschappelijk?, *NJB* 2004, 1416; N. HOEKX, K. VANHOVE and A. VERBEKE, "Yes we care! Bedenkingen over de (methode der) rechtswetenschap", *RW* 2008–09, 1786.

276 R.A.J VAN GESTEL, Preadvies "Kwaliteit van juridische publicaties. Over ranking, peer review, sciëntometrics en vertrouwen in alternatieve evaluatiemethoden" in NEDERLANDSE JURISTEN-VERENIGING, *Kwaliteit als keuze in rechtspraak, wetgeving en rechtswetenschap*, Deventer, Kluwer, 2015, 339.

3.5 METHODOLOGICAL FEATURES OF AN EXPLANATORY RESEARCH OBJECTIVE

An explanatory research objective aims to find an explanation for the enactment, alteration, abolishment or current problems of a legal construct. In this section we distinguish between an internal and an external approach for explanation.

3.5.1 INTERNAL APPROACH

When pursuing an explanatory research objective, legal scholars can opt for an internal approach. This approach looks for explanations within the existing structure and hierarchy of the legal system. First of all, it is possible to trace hierarchic higher rules or underlying principles of law that prescribe or influence a specific legal provision.[277] Examples are: the principle of equality guaranteed in national constitutions or the freedom of movement of services set forth in the TFEU.

Second, it is possible to consult preparatory works, case law and legal doctrine in order to discover the reasons or motives that led to the creation or alteration of a legal rule. Sometimes legal scholars can even look back at old(er) regulations or legal systems which might explain the current state of the art.[278] In those cases, however, it is important to realize that current legal concepts or constructs might not (yet) exist (in their current form) in previous times. For example: researchers who want to look into older Dutch legislation on the reintegration of benefit recipients and unemployed persons should be aware that the concept 'reintegration' did not exist 20 years ago. At that time, it was addressed as 'rehabilitation' or 'revalidation'.[279]

3.5.2 EXTERNAL APPROACH

Legal scholars may decide to explain the existence or the content of a legal rule on the basis of information *external* to the legal system. This will require the use of other academic disciplines and their knowledge, such as social sciences, history, psychology, economics, etc.[280] Indeed, social-historical factors can be

277 M. VAN HOECKE, "Hoe wetenschappelijk is de rechtswetenschap?", *TPR* 2009, 649; M. VAN HOECKE, "Legal Doctrine: Which Method(s) for What Kind of Discipline?" in M. VAN HOECKE (ed.), *Methodologies of Legal Research*, Oxford, Hart Publishing, 2011, 15.

278 L. KESTEMONT, *Naar een rechtswetenschappelijke methodeleer. Een expliciet methodologisch kader voor rechtswetenschappelijk onderzoek in het socialezekerheidsrecht*, Bruges, die Keure (reeks Begasoz/ Abetrass), 2017, 144.

279 Example from the meta-study of 45 PhDs on social security law: K.A. FABER, *Re-integratie volgens plan. Een onderzoek naar de mogelijkheden en consequenties van het gebruik van het instrument trajectplan bij re-integratie*, 2009, PhD University of Groningen.

280 M. VAN HOECKE, "Hoe wetenschappelijk is de rechtswetenschap?", *TPR* 2009, 649.

very helpful to explain legal changes, evolutions or patterns throughout a period of time.[281]

By opting for an external approach the research will become multi- or interdisciplinary.

3.6 METHODOLOGICAL FEATURES OF AN EVALUATIVE RESEARCH OBJECTIVE

An evaluative research objective aims to evaluate/assess legal constructs in view of a norm. In this section we discuss the selection of evaluation criteria, the difference between internal and external criteria and the operationalization of the selected criteria.

3.6.1 SELECTING EVALUATION CRITERIA

Every evaluation happens in view of a norm.[282] In this respect, legal scholars can assess the impact/influence of international rules on national legislation, the accessibility, transparency, quality or efficiency of a regulation, the degree to which legislation meets its objectives, the degree to which limitations to rights and freedoms can be justified, etc.[283] These norms will be reflected in a set of evaluation criteria. As different criteria may easily lead to a different outcome of the evaluation, it is important to clarify them.

Traditional legal scholars tend to use *internal* evaluation criteria, which are derived from the legal system itself and therefore result in an "assessment by reference to a standard set by law itself".[284] Examples are: legal rules, general principles of law, established case law or precedents, etc.[285] Internal criteria stress

---

281 M. SALTER and J. MASON, *Writing Law Dissertations*, Essex, Pearson, 2007, 195.

282 H. TIJSSEN, *De juridische dissertatie onder de loep*, The Hague, Boom Juridische uitgevers, 2009, 58.

283 L. KESTEMONT, *Naar een rechtswetenschappelijke methodeleer. Een expliciet methodologisch kader voor rechtswetenschappelijk onderzoek in het socialezekerheidsrecht*, Bruges, die Keure (series Begasoz/ Abetrass), 2017, 146 148.

284 R. CRYER, T. HERVEY and B. SOKHI-BULLEY, *Research Methodologies in EU and International Law*, Oxford, Hart Publishing, 2011, 10.

285 M. BARENDRECHT, J. VRANKEN, I. GIESEN, M.J. BORGERS, W. VAN DER BURG, H.E.B. TIJSSEN, G.C.G.J. VAN ROERMUND and W.H. VAN BOOM, "Methoden van rechtswetenschap: komen we verder?", *NJB* 2004, 1425; H. TIJSSEN, *De juridische dissertatie onder de loep*, The Hague, Boom Juridische uitgevers, 2009, 74; S. TAEKEMA en B. VAN KLINK, "On the Border. Limits and Possibilities of Interdisciplinary Research" in S. TAEKEMA en B. VAN KLINK (eds.), *Law and Method*, Tübingen, Mohr Siebeck, 2011, 22; G. VAN DIJCK, *Kwaliteit van de juridische annotatie*, The Hague, Boom Juridische uitgevers, 2011, 79; B.M.J. VAN KLINK and L.M. POORT, "De normativiteit van de rechtswetenschap", *RM Themis* 2013, 262.

the systematics, coherence and internal logics of a legal system.[286] An evaluation entirely based on internal criteria will therefore always have a purely legal character. However, non-legal knowledge may sometimes be involved when, for example, the degree of 'legal certainty' or 'equality' (i.e. internal criteria derived from the legal system) is assessed by making reference to empirical facts or research results.[287]

External evaluation criteria are derived from outside the legal system and will result in an "assessment by reference to an external standard."[288] External criteria may, for example, focus on the economic impact of legislation, the psychological impact of mediation or a cost-benefit analysis.[289] When applying external criteria, legal scholars have to include (knowledge of) other academic disciplines.[290] After all, determining whether the freeze of rental prizes brings along any economical (side) effects is not possible by simply using the common sense of a legal scholar.[291]

The selection of evaluation criteria depends on several factors. First of all, the substantive law concerned. As an example we can refer to researchers who want to evaluate the shift from public law to private law in social security schemes. They could consider 'transparency', 'consistency' and 'finality' as evaluation criteria, as these aspects will most likely come under pressure in the case of a shift from public to private law.[292] Second– and depending on the topic –, legal scholars may decide to use evaluation criteria that are already established in legislation, case law, legal doctrine or other instruments of (legal) bodies. They can, for example, derive their criteria from jurisprudence of the CJEU or from well-established legal doctrine.[293] Finally, the evaluation criteria can be

---

286 F. KUNNEMAN, *Rechtswetenschap*, Nijmegen, Ars Aequi Libri, 1991, 9.

287 See results of a meta-study of 45 PhDs on social security law: L. KESTEMONT, *Naar een rechtswetenschappelijke methodeleer. Een expliciet methodologisch kader voor rechtswetenschappelijk onderzoek in het socialezekerheidsrecht,* Bruges, die Keure (reeks Begasoz/ Abetrass), 2017, 204.

288 R. CRYER, T. HERVEY and B. SOKHI-BULLEY, *Research Methodologies in EU and International Law*, Oxford, Hart Publishing, 2011, 10.

289 M. BARENDRECHT, J. VRANKEN, I. GIESEN, M.J. BORGERS, W. VAN DER BURG, H.E.B. TIJSSEN, G.C.G.J. VAN ROERMUND and W.H. VAN BOOM, "Methoden van rechtswetenschap: komen we verder?", *NJB* 2004, 1426; F. KUNNEMAN, *Rechtswetenschap*, Nijmegen, Ars Aequi Libri, 1991, 9; H. TIJSSEN, *De juridische dissertatie onder de loep*, The Hague, Boom Juridische uitgevers, 2009, 75.

290 M. BARENDRECHT, J. VRANKEN, I. GIESEN, M.J. BORGERS, W. VAN DER BURG, H.E.B. TIJSSEN, G.C.G.J. VAN ROERMUND and W.H. VAN BOOM, "Methoden van rechtswetenschap: komen we verder?", *NJB* 2004, 1426; B.M.J. VAN KLINK and L.M. POORT, "De normativiteit van de rechtswetenschap", *RM Themis* 2013, 262.

291 Example from: M. VAN HOECKE, *Is de rechtswetenschap een empirische wetenschap?*, The Hague, Boom Juridische uitgevers, 2010, 41.

292 Example from the meta-study of 45 PhDs on social security law: A.M.P RIJPKEMA, *Toegang tot het recht bij ziekte en arbeidsongeschiktheid. Procedures en rechtsbescherming in de publiek-private mix*, 2013, PhD University of Groningen.

293 L. KESTEMONT, *Naar een rechtswetenschappelijke methodeleer. Een expliciet methodologisch kader voor rechtswetenschappelijk onderzoek in het socialezekerheidsrecht,* Bruges, die Keure (reeks Begasoz/ Abetrass), 2017, 148–149.

based on underlying legal-ethical premises on human dignity, solidarity or the constitutional state. Such premises are closely linked to the researcher's *frame of reference*, which is shaped throughout the years, not only by the researcher's education and national legal system or society, but also by his own opinions and personal beliefs. In part 4 of this handbook we go more deeply into the *researcher's frame of reference.*

3.6.2 OPERATIONALIZING EVALUATION CRITERIA

After selecting the evaluation criteria it is up to the researchers to operationalize them. This operationalization will result in an assessment framework.[294] Firstly, researchers have to clarify the selected criteria.[295] After all, these criteria will often refer to general principles of law (*legal certainty)* or open norms (*in the best interest of the child*) which lack a universal meaning, as they are restricted to a specific time and context.[296] It is therefore the researcher's responsibility to clarify their exact scope and meaning within the research project.

Secondly, researchers need to indicate how the evaluation will proceed: on the basis of which indicators and why?[297] For example: researchers want to evaluate a law according to its 'suitability' and determine that 'complexity of the law' will serve as a negative indicator for the evaluation. In this case, the researchers do not only have to clarify *why* the complexity of the law is considered to be a negative indicator, but they also have to elucidate *which degree of complexity* is (un)acceptable.[298] The same is true for an evaluation based on 'legal certainty': the researchers involved have to explain which indicators were used to decide whether there is 'more or less legal certainty'.[299]

---

294 H. TIJSSEN, *De juridische dissertatie onder de loep*, The Hague, Boom Juridische uitgevers, 2009, 74.

295 N. HOEKX, K. VANHOVE and A. VERBEKE, "Yes we care! Bedenkingen over de (methode der) rechtswetenschap", *RW* 2008–09, 1786; H. TIJSSEN, De juridische dissertatie onder de loep: de verantwoording van methodologische keuzes in juridische dissertaties, The Hague, Boom Juridische uitgevers, 2009, 75; M. HERWEIJER, "Juridisch onderzoek" in J.W.L. BROEKSTEEG and E.F. STAMHUIS (eds.), *Rechtswetenschappelijk onderzoek. Over object en methode*, The Hague, Boom Juridische uitgevers, 2003, 28; J.M. SMITS, *The Mind and Method of the Legal Academic*, Cheltenham, Edward Elgar, 2012, 115.

296 With respect to opne norms: see P.A. FRUYTIER, "Enkele beschouwingen over de interdisciplinaire rechtswetenschap. Braudel als uitgangspunt van een afbakening?", *AA* 2007, 834.

297 H. TIJSSEN, *De juridische dissertatie onder de loep*, The Hague, Boom Juridische uitgevers, 2009, 75, 110 and 187.

298 E. BREMS, "Methods in Legal Human Rights Research" in F. COOMANS, F. GRÜNFELD and T. KAMMINGA, *Methods of Human Rights Research*, Antwerp, Intersentia, 2009, 89.

299 H. TIJSSEN, *De juridische dissertatie onder de loep*, The Hague, Boom Juridische uitgevers, 2009, 75.

Thirdly, when operationalizing evaluation criteria legal scholars are confronted with their respective *weight:* how do the selected criteria relate to each other and which criteria have priority over the other?[300] Evaluation criteria can never have an absolute scope. First of all, every evaluation takes place in a specific context. This context may influence the evaluation in such a way that using the same evaluation criteria (e.g. 'transparency', 'consistency' and 'finality') in a different context or on a different level can lead to a different outcome.[301] Second, the outcome of an evaluation always depends on the respective weight of the evaluation criteria. In this respect, researchers may decide that in the case of a conflict between an internal and an external criterion, the internal criterion takes priority.[302] The opposite is also possible: when pursuing an evaluation on the basis of three internal criteria and only one external criterion (e.g. deterrent effect of a legal rule), researchers can decide to give more weight to the external criterion.

Finally, do evaluation criteria need to be selected and operationalized before the actual research has started, e.g. in a research proposal? Although it is advisable to already consider potential evaluation criteria in advance, legal scholars can decide to spend a part of their research to the selection and operationalization of the criteria. So although the evaluation criteria need to be set and operationalized before the actual evaluation, the process of selecting and operationalizing these criteria can be a part of the research itself.[303]

3.7 METHODOLOGICAL FEATURES OF A RECOMMENDATORY RESEARCH OBJECTIVE

A recommendatory research objective aims to formulate recommendations on how the law *should* be. This section will elaborate on the importance of a prior explanation and evaluation of the subject matter, on the selection of normative criteria and their distinction with evaluation criteria, on the operationalization of normative criteria, on the process of weighing (internal, external and comparative) criteria, and finally we will set out some guidelines for the formulation of recommendations.

---

300 VAN DIJCK refers to principles: G. VAN DIJCK, *Kwaliteit van de juridische annotatie,* The Hague, Boom Juridische uitgevers, 2011, 83. See also: H. TIJSSEN, *De juridische dissertatie onder de loep,* The Hague, Boom Juridische uitgevers, 2009, 110.

301 L. KESTEMONT, *Naar een rechtswetenschappelijke methodeleer. Een expliciet methodologisch kader voor rechtswetenschappelijk onderzoek in het socialezekerheidsrecht,* Bruges, die Keure (series Begasoz/ Abetrass), 2017, 152.

302 I. GIESEN, "The Use and Incorporation of Extralegal Insights in Legal Reasoning", *Utrecht Law Review* 2015, 15.

303 Results of a meta-study of 45 PhDs on social security law: L. KESTEMONT, *Naar een rechtswetenschappelijke methodeleer. Een expliciet methodologisch kader voor rechtswetenschappelijk onderzoek in het socialezekerheidsrecht,* Bruges, die Keure (series Begasoz/ Abetrass), 2017, 150.

3.7.1 PRELIMINARY DESCRIPTION, EXPLANATION AND EVALUATION

Prior to formulating recommendations, researchers first have to describe the subject matter, evaluate it, and explain the current problems.[304] This way the existing problems are not only mentioned, but also clarified: why do they exist?[305] This is essential information when wanting to formulate recommendations for improvement.[306]

Prior to formulating their own recommendations, legal scholars tend to look for inspiration in various places: (i) already existing proposals or recommendations, (ii) the past, being aware that old solutions or mechanisms do not always work in the present, (iii) the results of an internal or external comparison, (iv) or knowledge from other scientific disciplines.[307] In the latter case, the research will adopt a multi- or interdisciplinary approach.

3.7.2 SELECTING NORMATIVE CRITERIA

Recommendations on how the law *should* be are based on normative criteria selected by the researcher. If these criteria are not made explicit, the recommendations are not necessarily wrong or inadmissible as regards to their content.[308] However, they fall short from a methodological point of view because their underlying foundation was not clarified. Moreover, explicit normative criteria contribute to the repeatability of the (results of a) recommendatory research objective.[309] Explicit normative criteria also urge readers to look at the recommendations from the perspective of the researcher who made them, instead of putting forward their own criteria.[310]

Similar as to the evaluation criteria, a legal scholar can choose between internal or external normative criteria. Internal criteria are derived from the legal system itself and concern legal rights, duties, principles, guarantees,

304 H. TIJSSEN, *De juridische dissertatie onder de loep*, The Hague, Boom Juridische uitgevers, 2009, 59; R.A.J. VAN GESTEL and J.B.M. VRANKEN, "Rechtswetenschappelijke artikelen", *NJB* 2007, 1454.

305 Also HUTCHINSON beliefs that identifying the problem is the first step of '*law reform research*': T. HUTCHINSON, *Researching and writing in law*, Sydney, Lawbook Co., 2006, 58.

306 See also: R.A.J. VAN GESTEL and J.B.M. VRANKEN, "Rechtswetenschappelijke artikelen", *NJB* 2007, 1454.

307 L. KESTEMONT, *Naar een rechtswetenschappelijke methodeleer. Een expliciet methodologisch kader voor rechtswetenschappelijk onderzoek in het socialezekerheidsrecht*, Bruges, die Keure (reeks Begasoz/ Abetrass), 2017, 156–158.

308 R.A.J. VAN GESTEL and J.B.M. VRANKEN, "Rechtswetenschappelijke artikelen", *NJB* 2007, 1458.

309 See: G. VAN DIJCK, *Kwaliteit van de juridische annotatie*, The Hague, Boom Juridische uitgevers, 2011, 82.

310 P.C. KISSAM, "The evaluation of legal scholarship", *Wash.L.Rev.* 1998, 251.

procedures, etc. Legal scholars can choose to use criteria that were already applied in legislation, case law, legal doctrine or other (legal) documents. Recommendations solely based on internal criteria are of a purely legal nature.

External criteria are derived from outside the legal system. Examples are: the optimal protection of non-financial interests of victims, the stimulation of entrepreneurship or the reduction of health care costs.[311] The use of external criteria turns a traditional legal research into a multi- or interdisciplinary research.

The selection of normative criteria will depend on the researcher, as "what ought to be done would not be a matter of facts that are the same for everybody, but a matter of taste, or choice, which may have a different outcome for different persons even if they are all fully rational."[312] Two legal scholars working on the same research can put forward a different recommendation at the end of the research.[313] One researcher can highly value a traditional viewpoint in legal doctrine, whereas the other one can be led by new insights from law-and-economics.

In sum, recommendations on how the law *should* be are based on normative criteria, and these criteria will always depend on the researcher who selects them.[314] However, the latter does not allow legal scholars to formulate recommendations according to their own personal feeling without any further clarification. On the contrary, recommendations are part of the research and need to be presented to the academic community for verification. For that purpose, the normative criteria underlying the recommendations have to be made explicit.

The *researcher's frame of reference* will play a significant role in the selection of normative criteria. We go more deeply into this concept in part 4 of the handbook.

3.7.3 FROM EVALUATION TO RECOMMENDATION: THE NEED FOR NORMATIVE CRITERIA

The normative criteria set forth to formulate recommendations can to some extent correspond to the criteria used for the preceding evaluation. After all, researchers' preferences – determined by their personal *frame of reference* – stay the same whether they reflect on evaluation criteria or normative criteria. This,

311 L. ALEXANDER, "What We Do, and Why We Do it", *Stan.L.Rev.* 1993, 1887; M. BARENDRECHT, J. VRANKEN, I. GIESEN, M.J. BORGERS, W. VAN DER BURG, H.E.B. TIJSSEN, G.C.G.J. VAN ROERMUND and W.H. VAN BOOM, "Methoden van rechtswetenschap: komen we verder?", *NJB* 2004, 1425.

312 J. HAGE, "The Method of a Truly Normative Legal Science" in M. VAN HOECKE (ed.), *Methodologies of Legal Research*, Oxford, Hart Publishing, 2011, 30. See also: F. KUNNEMAN, *Rechtswetenschap*, Nijmegen, Ars Aequi Libri, 1991, 8; C.H. SIEBURGH, "L'art de la distinction", *NJB* 2008, 3–4.

313 P. SCHOLTEN, "De structuur der rechtswetenschap" in *Verzamelde Geschriften van wijlen Prof. Mr. Paul Scholten*, Zwolle, Tjeenk Willink, 1949, 462.

314 F. KUNNEMAN, *Rechtswetenschap*, Nijmegen, Ars Aequi Libri, 1991, 8.

however, does not mean that legal scholars can jump from (positive or negative) evaluation results to the formulation of their recommendations.[315] A separate set of normative criteria remains necessary.

First of all, the results of an evaluation rarely point out one clear direction. It is, for example, possible that an evaluation assesses several proposals of law as 'positive'. This evaluation result, however, is not able to indicate which proposal of law is preferable to the other. In order to make that kind of recommendation, additional normative criteria are necessary.[316]

Second, an evaluation only aims to assess a legal construct: positive/negative, advantageous/disadvantageous, violation/no violation, etc. These assessments do not as such indicate which changes or adjustments *should* be made to improve the law.[317] Again, additional normative criteria are necessary in order to formulate such kinds of recommendations.

Third, although intending to use the same evaluation and normative criteria, legal scholars may decide after their evaluation to adapt the original criteria before formulating recommendations. For example: choosing a more lenient/strict interpretation of the proportionality criterion or refining the criterion 'improving the legal status of tenants' to 'improving the legal status of tenants with consideration of the protection of third parties'. This way normative criteria will have their own scope and meaning, and will differ from the evaluation criteria.

3.7.4 OPERATIONALIZING NORMATIVE CRITERIA

Legal scholars do not only have to make their normative criteria explicit[318], but they also have to clarify their meaning and scope.[319] After all, these criteria often refer to general legal principles (*equality*), general concepts (*solidarity)* or open norms (*human treatment).* Because such principles, concepts and norms

---

315 However, TIJSSEN states that legal scholars make this jump very often. See: H. TIJSSEN, *De juridische dissertatie onder de loep*, The Haugue, Boom Juridische uitgevers, 2009, 183.

316 L. KESTEMONT, "A Meta-Methodological Study of Dutch and Belgian PhDs on Social Security Law: Devising a Typology of Research Objectives as a Supporting Tool", *E.J.S.S.* 2015, 378.

317 L. KESTEMONT, "A Meta-Methodological Study of Dutch and Belgian PhDs on Social Security Law: Devising a Typology of Research Objectives as a Supporting Tool", *E.J.S.S.* 2015, 378.

318 N. HOEKX, K. VANHOVE en A. VERBEKE, "Yes we care! Bedenkingen over de (methode der) rechtswetenschap", *RW* 2008–09, 1786; M. BARENDRECHT, J. VRANKEN, I. GIESEN, M.J. BORGERS, W. VAN DER BURG, H.E.B. TIJSSEN, G.C.G.J. VAN ROERMUND en W.H. VAN BOOM, "Methoden van rechtswetenschap: komen we verder?", *NJB* 2004, 1426; C.J.J.M. STOLKER, "Ja, geléérd zijn jullie wel!", 2003, https://openaccess.leidenuniv.nl/handle/1887/3727, 8; E.M. MEIJERS, *Dogmatische rechtswetenschap,* 's-Gravenhage, Belinfante, 1903, 50; E.L. RUBIN, "The Practice and Discourse of Legal Scholarship", *Mich.L.Rev.* 1987–88, 1851 en 1893; A. SOETEMAN, "Wetenschappelijke rechtsgeleerdheid", *R & R* 2009, 234; R.A.J. VAN GESTEL en J.B.M. VRANKEN, "Rechtswetenschappelijke artikelen", *NJB* 2007, 1458.

319 J. SINGER, "Normative Methods for Lawyers", *Harvard Law School Public Law Research Paper No. 08-05*, 2008, 23.

are restricted to a specific time and context[320], researchers have to clarify their content within the specific research project.

Legal scholars need to motivate why they have chosen the particular normative criteria. This demand for motivation and justification will make researchers more conscious of their personal preferences, as "the more one's own position (viewpoints, dogmas, bias, etc.) are recognized, the more potential counter-arguments will matter (as it is more clear that they conflict with each other), and the more the final decision will be determined by balancing arguments, rather than one's own bias."[321]

Finally, also with respect to normative criteria the question arises whether they have to be set and operationalized before the actual research, e.g. in a research proposal. Although it is advisable to consider normative criteria in advance – as they determine the perspective of the research – it is possible to spend a part of the actual research on their selection and operationalization. In other words, the criteria have to be determined and operationalized before formulating recommendations; however, the process of selecting and operationalizing can be a part of the research itself.[322]

3.7.5 PROCESS OF BALANCING CRITERIA

The scope, the indicators and the respective weight of the normative criteria will be essential for the process of formulating recommendations. Also balancing these criteria will be important.

3.7.5.1 Balancing internal normative criteria

Legal scholars cannot use internal criteria on automatic pilot, as they often embody legal rights and principles whose relationship can be rather tense. Moreover, during the research legal scholars can be confronted with rights and principles that were not included in their own normative criteria.[323] Jurists are therefore trained

---

320 Regarding the 'open norms' see: P.A. FRUYTIER, "Enkele beschouwingen over de interdisciplinaire rechtswetenschap. Braudel als uitgangspunt van een afbakening?", *AA* 2007, 834.

321 Translation of: "naarmate de eigen positie (standpunt, dogma's, vooringenomenheid enz.) duidelijker wordt onderkend, doen eventuele contra-argumenten er meer toe (het is duidelijker dat ze botsen) en zal men de eindbeslissing meer laten bepalen door de weging van argumenten dan door eigen vooringenomenheid." C.J.J.M. STOLKER, "Ja, geléérd zijn jullie wel!", 2003, https://openaccess.leidenuniv.nl/handle/1887/3727, 13.

322 L. KESTEMONT, *Naar een rechtswetenschappelijke methodeleer. Een expliciet methodologisch kader voor rechtswetenschappelijk onderzoek in het socialezekerheidsrecht*, Bruges, die Keure (reeks Begasoz/ Abetrass), 2017, 219.

323 HERWEIJER refers to an "area of tension". M. HERWEIJER, "Juridisch onderzoek" in J.W.L. BROEKSTEEG and E.F. STAMHUIS (eds.), *Rechtswetenschappelijk onderzoek. Over object en methode*, The Hague, Boom Juridische uitgevers, 2003, 31.

to balance different arguments, values, principles, viewpoints and interests.[324] This practice of balancing, where in the end researchers value one legal principle or rule higher than the other, is important when formulating recommendations.[325]

The way researchers deal with conflicting legal principles or rules will depend on the particular context. It is, for example, possible to interpret conflicting principles in such a way that they do no longer fundamentally contradict or exclude each other.[326] Restricting the scope or effects of one principle can leave room for another, this way eliminating the original conflict. However, if the conflict is irreconcilable, it is up to the researcher to determine which principle is subordinate to the other.[327]

3.7.5.2 Balancing external normative criteria

Legal scholars can use external normative criteria to formulate recommendations. However, external criteria are as such insufficient to recommend how the law *should* be.[328] For example: the results of a law-and-economics research into the financial consequences of damages in case of lawful government actions cannot as such make recommendations on the desirability of such compensation schemes.[329] Or psychological research explaining that "warning signs are only followed by those people who have been given the warning if the costs of complying with that warning are low" cannot simply lead to the recommendation that "a legal duty to warn should be rejected, as being superfluous, in all other circumstances."[330] It is possible that (internal) legal arguments point in a different direction.[331] Legal scholars who use external

---

324 J.B.M. VRANKEN, "Een nieuw rechtsrealisme in het privaatrecht", *WPNR* 2011, 1121; E. VAN DAMME, "Verwevenheid van recht en economie" in M. GROENHUIJSEN, E. HONDIUS and A. SOETEMAN (eds.), *Recht in Geding*, The Hague, Boom Juridische uitgeverij, 2014, 259.

325 M. VAN HOECKE, "Legal Doctrine: Which Method(s) for What Kind of Discipline?" in M. VAN HOECKE (ed.), *Methodologies of Legal Research*, Oxford, Hart Publishing, 2011, 10.

326 J. SINGER, "Normative Methods for Lawyers", *Harvard Law School Public Law Research Paper No. 08-05*, 2008, 74.

327 J. SINGER, "Normative Methods for Lawyers", *Harvard Law School Public Law Research Paper No. 08-05*, 2008, 74.

328 E.L. RUBIN, "Law and the Methodology of Law", *Wis.L.Rev.* 1997, 545–546 and 554; G. DE GEEST, "Hoe maken we van de rechtswetenschap een volwaardige wetenschap?", *NJB* 2004, 60; R. VAN GESTEL and H.-W. MICKLITZ, "Revitalising Doctrinal Legal Research in Europe: What About Methodology?" in U. NEERGAARD, R. NIELSEN and L. ROSEBERRY (eds.), *European Legal Method – Paradoxes and Revitalisation*, Kopenhagen, DJØF Publishing, 2011, 64.

329 R.A.J. VAN GESTEL and J.B.M. VRANKEN, "Rechtswetenschappelijke artikelen", *NJB* 2007, 1457.

330 I. GIESEN, "The Use and Incorporation of Extralegal Insights in Legal Reasoning", *Utrecht Law Review* 2015, 2.

331 See also: S. TAEKEMA and B. VAN KLINK, "On the Border. Limits and Possibilities of Interdisciplinary Research" in S. TAEKEMA and B. VAN KLINK (eds.), *Law and Method*, Tübingen, Mohr Siebeck, 2011, 18.

criteria should therefore always go back to the rules, procedures, values and legal principles of the legal system itself.[332]

When applying non-legal knowledge legal scholars should refrain from referring only to (empirical) findings that confirm or support their own argument.[333] This relates to the problem of "concealed arguing", i.e. presenting arguments in such a way that they prevent an undesirable outcome and lead to the result the researcher had in mind from the start.[334] This practice was already condemned by legal doctrine in the case of *legal* arguments; however, it is also impermissible when using insights from other academic disciplines.

As non-legal insights cannot simply be transposed into the legal system, VRANKEN clarifies that a "translation" is necessary.[335] Such translation will determine the meaning of non-legal insights in the discourse of the legal scholar, giving them their own spot in the balancing process, next to the traditional legal principles, values, arguments, viewpoints and interests.[336]

According to GIESEN, legal doctrine largely ignores the 'translation' issue or simply refers to it without providing a solution.[337] He looked at comparative law for further inspiration: the fact that one legal construct is working well in legal system A is as such insufficient to conclude that legal system B *should* adopt the same legal construct. After all, this concerns a normative choice for which legal arguments (including the comparative argument) are balanced, weighed against each other.[338] GIESEN wonders whether this praxis in the case of *two different legal systems* could be helpful for the translation process in the case of *two different academic disciplines*.[339] This would imply that the empirical argument (i.e. fact or information belonging to another discipline than legal scholarship) is included in the whole collection of arguments, which are balanced in order to decide on the recommendations.[340] This way non-legal insights can contribute

---

332 B.M.J. VAN KLINK and L.M. POORT, "De normativiteit van de rechtswetenschap", *RM Themis* 2013, 266.

333 F.L. LEEUW, "Empirical Legal Research: The Gap between Facts and Values and Legal Academic Training", *Utrecht Law Review* 2015, 23.

334 Translation of: "verhullend argumenteren" J.B.M. VRANKEN, "Algemeen Deel. Een synthese" in *Mr. C. Assers Handleiding tot de beoefening van het Nederlands Burgerlijk Recht*, Deventer, Kluwer, 2014, 17.

335 J.B.M. VRANKEN, "Algemeen Deel. Een synthese" in *Mr. C. Assers Handleiding tot de beoefening van het Nederlands Burgerlijk Recht*, Deventer, Kluwer, 2014, 28.

336 J.B.M. VRANKEN, "Algemeen Deel. Een synthese" in *Mr. C. Assers Handleiding tot de beoefening van het Nederlands Burgerlijk Recht*, Deventer, Kluwer, 2014, 189; J.B.M. VRANKEN, "Een nieuw rechtsrealisme in het privaatrecht", *WPNR* 2011, 1121.

337 See for a literature overview: I. GIESEN, "The Use and Incorporation of Extralegal Insights in Legal Reasoning", *Utrecht Law Review* 2015, 4–11.

338 I. GIESEN, "The Use and Incorporation of Extralegal Insights in Legal Reasoning", *Utrecht Law Review* 2015, 14.

339 I. GIESEN, "The Use and Incorporation of Extralegal Insights in Legal Reasoning", *Utrecht Law Review* 2015, 14.

340 GIESEN explicitly refers to VRANKEN. See: I. GIESEN, "Het incorporeren van extrajuridische inzichten in het privaatrechtelijke debat" in G. VAN DIJCK, R. VAN

to the formulation of recommendations while at the same time being weighed against the legal arguments.[341] This praxis would correspond to the fact that law has its own normative frameworks, requiring that non-legal knowledge is balanced with law's own rules (of play), principles and values.[342]

The abovementioned praxis gives the 'translation' of non-legal knowledge a case-by-case basis[343], for which GIESEN proposes a "due process approach". He makes a non-exhaustive list of criteria in order to test the non-legal knowledge before actually using it:

- "whether the empirical work is in fact relevant for the question of law that arises,
- whether the work is up to the current state of the art in the field methodologically, as well as regards its research design, etc., and its implications,
- whether (more generally) the research is valid and reliable,
- whether there is conflicting empirical work on the same issue,
- whether the study has been replicated and confirmed or not,
- whether the study is but one building block of a larger set of studies needed for policy implications,
- whether the researcher is both an expert and objective and independent, and so on."[344]

If non-legal knowledge meets these criteria, it can be considered as an argument in the balancing process.[345] During that process it will become clear whether or not the non-legal (external) arguments will be overruled by other (internal) arguments.[346] In the end, it is up to the researcher to motivate why non-legal arguments were (not) pursued.

Although the due process approach is convincing, LEEUW complains that it does not tackle the actual problem, namely "leaping from valid (and

---

GESTEL, I. GIESEN and F. HAMMERSTEIN (red.), *Cirkels. Een terugblik op een vooruitziende blik*, Deventer, Kluwer, 2013, 227.

341 See also: J. SMITS, "Law and Interdisciplinarity: On the Inevitable Normativity of Legal Studies, *Critical Analysis of Law* 2014, 85.

342 I. GIESEN, "Het incorporeren van extrajuridische inzichten in het privaatrechtelijke debat" in G. VAN DIJCK, R. VAN GESTEL, I. GIESEN and F. HAMMERSTEIN (red.), *Cirkels. Een terugblik op een vooruitziende blik*, Deventer, Kluwer, 2013, 228–229; T.R. ROUX, "The Incorporation Problem in Interdisciplinary Legal Research: Some Conceptual Issues and a Practical Illustration", *SSRN* 2014, 8.

343 I. GIESEN, "The Use and Incorporation of Extralegal Insights in Legal Reasoning", *Utrecht Law Review* 2015, 14. Also VRANKEN claims that there is no "one size fits all answer": J.B.M. VRANKEN, "Algemeen Deel. Een synthese" in *Mr. C. Assers Handleiding tot de beoefening van het Nederlands Burgerlijk Recht*, Deventer, Kluwer, 2014, 196.

344 I. GIESEN, "The Use and Incorporation of Extralegal Insights in Legal Reasoning", *Utrecht Law Review* 2015, 16.

345 I. GIESEN, "The Use and Incorporation of Extralegal Insights in Legal Reasoning", *Utrecht Law Review* 2015, 16–17.

346 I. GIESEN, "The Use and Incorporation of Extralegal Insights in Legal Reasoning", *Utrecht Law Review* 2015, 16 and 18.

relevant) empirical evidence (compliant with due process criteria or the Daubert standard) to formulating normative statements."[347] Although legal doctrine is acknowledging the 'translation' issue, a clear answer or a common approach remains absent.[348]

3.7.5.3 Balancing results of comparative studies

The results of comparative law can be interesting and inspiring for the formulation of recommendations. After all, they indicate how other legal systems deal with similar problems.[349] In SMITS' "empirical-normative approach" comparative law even plays an essential role.[350] According to him, *how the law should be* is an ongoing subject for debate. Legal scholars should therefore continuously look for arguments, balance them and indicate how they could fit into a specific legal system.[351] For this praxis, other legal systems play an important role, as they can be considered as "laboratories for dealing with conflicting normative arguments. They show which arguments exist in favour of, and against, any particular solution, which arguments have prevailed elsewhere and how the result has been received in that jurisdiction."[352]

Despite the usefulness of comparative results, they are a relatively weak basis for formulating recommendations.[353] It is not because foreign solutions are more efficient or appear in different legal systems that a national legal system should (literally) copy these solutions.[354] On the contrary, borrowing a foreign

---

347 F.L. LEEUW, "Empirical Legal Research: The Gap between Facts and Values and Legal Academic Training", *Utrecht Law Review* 2015, 26.

348 E. VAN DAMME, "Verwevenheid van recht en economie" in M. GROENHUIJSEN, E. HONDIUS and A. SOETEMAN (eds.), *Recht in Geding*, The Hague, Boom Juridische uitgeverij, 2014, 274.

349 M. HERWEIJER, "Juridisch onderzoek" in J.W.L. BROEKSTEEG and E.F. STAMHUIS (eds.), *Rechtswetenschappelijk onderzoek. Over object en methode*, The Hague, Boom Juridische uitgevers, 2003, 31; M. SALTER and J. MASON, *Writing Law Dissertations*, Essex, Pearson, 2007, 183; J.C. REITZ, "How to Do Comparative Law?", *Am.J.Comp.L.* 1998, 624.

350 For more information; see: J.M. SMITS, *The Mind and Method of the Legal Academic*, Cheltenham, Edward Elgar, 2012, 180 p. or J. SMITS, *Omstreden Rechtswetenschap: over aard, methode en organisatie van de juridische discipline*, The Hague, Boom Juridische uitgevers, 2009, 235 p.

351 J.M. SMITS, *The Mind and Method of the Legal Academic*, Cheltenham, Edward Elgar, 2012, 97.

352 J.M. SMITS, *The Mind and Method of the Legal Academic*, Cheltenham, Edward Elgar, 2012, 77.

353 J.C. REITZ, "How to Do Comparative Law?", *Am.J.Comp.L.* 1998, 624; R. MICHAELS, "The Functional Method of Comparative Law" in M. REIMANN and R. ZIMMERMANN (eds.), *The Oxford Handbook of Comparative Law*, Oxford, Oxford University Press, 2006, 374 and 379–380.

354 J.C. REITZ, "How to Do Comparative Law?", *Am.J.Comp.L.* 1998, 624–625; R. MICHAELS, "The Functional Method of Comparative Law" in M. REIMANN and R. ZIMMERMANN (eds.), *The Oxford Handbook of Comparative Law*, Oxford, Oxford University Press, 2006,

solution will fail if it contradicts the structure and fundaments of a national legal system.[355] As a matter of fact, the same is true for internal comparisons: legal scholars should be aware of the fundaments, principles, instruments and procedures of distinct areas of law.

Also national politics and socio-economic circumstances play an essential role.[356] A regulation – e.g. allowing unrestricted abortion – that has proven to be efficient to meet a specific goal – e.g. tempering the rise in population – will not work in a society that does not support abortion.[357] So legal scholars "should see more clearly whether and how far it is reasonable to borrow from other systems and from which systems, and whether it is possible to accept foreign solutions with modifications or without modifications".[358]

A foreign solution that does not seem to fit another legal system should not be abandoned right away. First of all, it is possible that foreign solutions can be applied to other legal systems if some small adjustments are made.[359] Second, a *non-matching* foreign solution can nevertheless incite national legal scholars to reflect on (the structure and fundaments of) their own legal system. The weak normative basis of comparative results does not imply that legal scholars should always formulate *conservative* recommendations that are "confirming and consolidating existing preconceptions about law and society."[360] Indeed, non-matching foreign solutions can contribute to a critical reflection on one's own legal system.[361]

374; D. PIETERS, "Functions of comparative law and practical methodology of comparing" in *Syllabus Research Master in Law*, Leuven-Tilburg, 2009, 31.

355 J.B.M. VRANKEN, "Algemeen Deel" in *Asser's Handleiding tot de beoefening van het Nederlands Burgerlijk Recht*, Zwolle, W.E.J. Tjeenk Willink, 1995, 124; J.C. REITZ, "How to Do Comparative Law?", *Am.J.Comp.L.* 1998, 624. SMITS discusses this in view of the normative arguments within a legal system: J.M. SMITS, *The Mind and Method of the Legal Academic*, Cheltenham, Edward Elgar, 2012, 94.

356 W. PINTENS, *Inleiding tot de rechtsvergelijking*, Leuven, Universitaire Pers Leuven, 1998, 92; J.B.M. VRANKEN, "Algemeen Deel" in *Asser's Handleiding tot de beoefening van het Nederlands Burgerlijk Recht*, Zwolle, W.E.J. Tjeenk Willink, 1995, 138; M. SIEMS, *Comparative Law*, Cambridge, Cambridge University Press, 2014, 23.

357 Based on SIEMS referring to an example of BOGDAN: M. SIEMS, *Comparative Law*, Cambridge, Cambridge University Press, 2014, 23.

358 A. WATSON, *Legal Transplants*, Edinburgh, Scottish Academic Press, 1974, 16. For an original perspective on legal transplants take a look at M.M. SIEMS, "The Curious Case of Overfitting Legal Transplants" in M. ADAMS and D. HEIRBAUT (eds.), *The Method and Culture of Comparative Law*, Oxford, Hart Publishing, 2014, 133–146.

359 J.C. REITZ, "How to Do Comparative Law?", *Am.J.Comp.L.* 1998, 625.

360 J. HILL, "Comparative Law, Law Reform and Legal Theory", *O.J.L.S.* 1989, 106.

361 J. HILL, "Comparative Law, Law Reform and Legal Theory", *O.J.L.S.* 1989, 107; M. SALTER and J. MASON, *Writing Law Dissertations*, Essex, Pearson, 2007, 189. Also PIETERS underlines how comparative law leads to a permanent critical attitude towards one's own legal system and national preconceptions: D. PIETERS, "Functions of comparative law and practical methodology of comparing" in *Syllabus Research Master in Law*, Leuven-Tilburg, 2009, 4.

3.7.6 FORMULATING RECOMMENDATIONS

3.7.6.1 *Different types of recommendations*

A legal scholar can formulate different types of recommendations.[362] *Specific recommendations* prescribe in detail what should happen with a specific legal construct, whereas *framework recommendations* set out general guidelines for policymakers who will draft legislation. *Facet recommendations* concentrate on specific aspects of a legal matter, whereas *global recommendations* tend to deal with the matter as a whole. Legal scholars can of course use a combination of types: e.g. first drafting a general framework and afterwards using it to formulate more specific recommendations, or first formulating recommendations on specific aspects of a legal matter and afterwards taking a more global approach.

A *hierarchical recommendation* formulates several recommendations in an order of ranking: (i) the ideal proposal, (ii) a compromise/moderate proposal, and (iii) a confined proposal. The idea is that policymakers should at least adopt the confined proposal, but at the same time they are encouraged to go a step further. Legal scholars can also opt for *multiple recommendations* when they intend to work out various scenarios or alternatives. Different options or variations are worked out and are presented with their pros and cons, without any order of ranking.

Finally, a *bipartite recommendation* consists of two layers: one layer puts forward 'requirements' that policymakers definitely have to comply with, whereas the second layer lists 'options' from which policymakers can choose when drafting their legislation.

3.7.6.2 *Transparent clarification of the proposed recommendations*

In the end, legal scholars will formulate recommendations on the basis of their selected normative criteria: what is the *best* solution, which alterations *should* be made? When clarifying and motivating their recommendations, legal scholars should be transparent. In the following we discuss two general guidelines in order to avoid that researchers give their own recommendation(s) an absolute range.[363]

First of all, one problem can be solved by different solutions.[364] In the end, the researcher will prefer one solution because "reasons of technical fit, social

362 Based on the results of a meta-study of 45 PhDs on social security law: L. KESTEMONT, *Naar een rechtswetenschappelijke methodeleer. Een expliciet methodologisch kader voor rechtswetenschappelijk onderzoek in het socialezekerheidsrecht,* Bruges, die Keure (series Begasoz/ Abetrass), 2017, 153–156.

363 The danger of absolutism was also addressed by TIJSSEN in H. TIJSSEN, *De juridische dissertatie onder de loep*, The Hague, Boom Juridische uitgevers, 2009, 49.

364 See for example: C.J.J.M. STOLKER, "Ja, geléérd zijn jullie wel!", 2003, https://openaccess.leidenuniv.nl/handle/1887/3727, 1–4.

consequence, and normative attractiveness."[365] In this respect, it is of utmost importance to clarify and motivate the choice made, instead of pretending that the recommendation is a logical consequence or outcome of the current legal system.[366]

Second, researchers cannot only refer to legal documents, case law or legal doctrine that support their recommendation(s). Such unilateral approach of using source material is focused on persuasion (typical of legal practice), rather than legal scholarship.[367] Also counter-arguments should be mentioned and addressed.[368] Moreover, every solution has its pros and cons. Legal scholars, however, tend to only shed light on the positive aspects of their recommendation.[369] Although legal practitioners (such as lawyers and judges) mainly focus on arguments that support their conclusions or judgments[370], legal scholars cannot adopt such a unilateral approach. Researchers also have to address the weaknesses, counter-arguments and undesired side effects of their recommendation(s).[371] Moreover, showing that the disadvantages and counter-arguments do not outweigh the positive aspects of the recommendation will strengthen both the argumentation and the recommendation.[372]

365 T.R. ROUX, "Judging the quality of legal research: A qualified response to the demand for greater methodological rigour", *SSRN* 2014, 9.

366 J.B.M. VRANKEN, "Algemeen Deel. Een synthese" in *Mr. C. Assers Handleiding tot de beoefening van het Nederlands Burgerlijk Recht,* Deventer, Kluwer, 2014, 199. See also: G. DE GEEST, "Hoe maken we van de rechtswetenschap een volwaardige wetenschap?", *NJB* 2004, 63.

367 T.F.E. TJONG TJIN TAI, "Verantwoording van bronnen" in G. VAN DIJCK, R. VAN GESTEL, I. GIESEN and F. HAMMERSTEIN (red.), *Cirkels. Een terugblik op een vooruitziende blik,* Deventer, Kluwer, 2013, 202–203.

368 J.B.M. VRANKEN, "Algemeen Deel. Een synthese" in *Mr. C. Assers Handleiding tot de beoefening van het Nederlands Burgerlijk Recht,* Deventer, Kluwer, 2014, 139.

369 M. VAN HOECKE, *Is de rechtswetenschap een empirische wetenschap?,* The Hague, Boom Juridische uitgevers, 2010, 35.

370 M. VAN HOECKE, *Is de rechtswetenschap een empirische wetenschap?,* The Hague, Boom Juridische uitgevers, 2010, 35.

371 N. HOEKX, K. VANHOVE and A. VERBEKE, "Yes we care! Bedenkingen over de (methode der) rechtswetenschap", *RW* 2008–09, 1786; J.M. SMITS, *The Mind and Method of the Legal Academic,* Cheltenham, Edward Elgar, 2012, 119; A.R. BLOEMBERGEN, "Iets over object en methode van wetenschap en rechtspraak in het privaatrecht" in O.W.M. KAMSTRA, F.B.M. KUNNEMAN and C.W. MARIS (eds.), *Nederlandse rechtswetenschap. Tussen distantie en betrokkenheid: paradigma's in de twintigste eeuw,* Zwolle, W.E.J. Tjeenk Willink, 1988, 77; B. VANGEEBERGEN and D. VAN DAELE, "Is de studie van het recht een wetenschap en wie kan het wat schelen?, *RW* 2009, 993.

372 M. BARENDRECHT, J. VRANKEN, I. GIESEN, M.J. BORGERS, W. VAN DER BURG, H.E.B. TIJSSEN, G.C.G.J. VAN ROERMUND en W.H. VAN BOOM, "Methoden van rechtswetenschap: komen we verder?", *NJB* 2004, 1426; I. CURRY-SUMNER, F. KIRSTEN, T. VAN DER LINDEN-SMITH en J. TIGCHELAAR, *Onderzoeksvaardigheden,* Nijmegen, Ars Aequi Libri, 2010, 38.

4 RESEARCH OBJECTIVES AND OVERALL METHODOLOGICAL FEATURES

Part 3 of this handbook describes how every type of research objective calls for its own specific methodological features. However, there are also some overall methodological features which are applicable to all research objectives. In the following we will discuss the importance of dissent, the possibility of interactions between different types of research objectives and the researcher's *frame of reference*.

4.1 ATTENTION FOR DISSENT

When discussing the methodological features of the theory-building and the recommendatory research objective, the importance of dissent was clearly mentioned: legal scholars cannot only refer to legal documents, case law or authors who support their theory or recommendation. It was argued that this kind of unilateral approach (focused on persuasion) is unacceptable for legal scholarship.

The attention for dissent, however, applies to all research objectives. When pursuing any research objective it is important for legal scholars to occasionally step away from their own way of thinking and to look for dissenting opinions, counter-arguments or conflicting interests. Instead of trying to hide dissent, legal scholars should embrace and address it: do other authors have a different opinion, why do they have a different opinion, why do we not share that opinion, etc.? Moreover, by explicitly dealing with counter-arguments and dissenting opinions legal scholars can strengthen their own arguments and mark their own spot within the academic community and its ongoing debate.

4.2 INTERACTION BETWEEN DIFFERENT RESEARCH OBJECTIVES – RESEARCH ISLANDS

Part 3 of this handbook has shown that every type of research objective has its own purpose and methodological features. However, during the research process these different types of objectives might closely interact with each other. The following passages were taken from the meta-study of our PhD project and they are concrete examples of how different types of research objectives can interact with each other. We refer in brackets to the research objectives involved.

Example 1:

"The systems involved in the comparison were studied *(descriptive)* and evaluated *(evaluative)* on equal terms.[...] In the end, the evaluations were brought into a comparative perspective *(comparative)* on the basis of which possible recommendations were formulated *(recommendatory).* "[1]

Example 2:

"This chapter will provide a description of the concept 'supplementary retirement or old-age pension for employees in the second pillar' *(descriptive)*. The description will be compared to existing definitions in relevant legislatives acts *(comparative)* in order to check by means of a confrontation *(evaluation)* whether the proposed definition should be adapted *(recommendatory)*."[2]

Example 3:

"In this chapter the central question is: 'What is the legal character of the development plan'? *(classifying)* In order to answer this question, both the characteristics *(descriptive)* and the differences *(comparative)* between a contract and an administrative decision will be discussed. In the introductory chapter the development plan was defined as follows: [...] This definition will be used to evaluate whether the instrument of a development plan meets the characteristics of a contract or an administrative decision *(evaluative)*.[3]

Example 4:

"In what follows, the attitude of the Belgian case law towards the principle of standstill will be examined. The case law of the Council of State, the Court of Cassation and the Constitutional Court will be discussed in chronological

---

1 Translation of: "De systemen die in de rechtsvergelijking werden betrokken, werden op voet van gelijkheid onderzocht en beoordeeld. [...] Ten slotte werden deze beoordelingen in rechtsvergelijkend perspectief geplaatst en werden op deze basis eventuele aanbevelingen geformuleerd." M. JANSSENS, *De rechtspositie van private zorgvoorzieningen in de residentiële ouderenzorg. Een rechtsvergelijkende analyse van de functioneringsvrijheid van private zorgvoorzieningen*, PhD KU Leuven, 2013.

2 Translation of: "In dit hoofdstuk wordt een omschrijving gegeven van het begrip 'aanvullende rust- of ouderdomspensioenen voor werknemers in de tweede pijler'. Deze omschrijving wordt vergeleken met bestaande definities in relevante wetgevende teksten om door de confrontatie na te gaan of de voorgestelde definitie moet worden aangepast." K. VERRETH, *Aanvullende sociale verzekeringen. Arbeidsmobiliteit en aanvullende pensioenen in België en Europa: een sociaalrechtelijke benadering*, PhD KU Leuven, 2000.

3 Translation of: "In dit hoofdstuk staat daarom de vraag centraal: 'Wat is het rechtskarakter van het trajectplan?' Om deze vraag te kunnen beantwoorden, zullen de kenmerken van en de verschillen tussen de rechtsfiguren contract en beschikking worden besproken. In het inleidende hoofdstuk is het trajectplan als volgt gedefinieerd: [...] Aan de hand van deze definitie zal worden beoordeeld of het instrument trajectplan aan de kenmerken van een contract voldoet of aan de kenmerken van een beschikking." K.A. FABER, *Re-integratie volgens plan. Een onderzoek naar de mogelijkheden en consequenties van het gebruik van het instrument trajectplan bij re-integratie*, PhD University of Groningen, 2009.

order *(descriptive)*. With this similarities and differences will be looked for *(comparative)*, in order to try to develop a general theory later on *(theory-building)*."[4]

All these passages – derived from existing PhDs – clearly show how different types of research objectives may interact during the research process. In large research projects, such as PhDs, these kinds of interactions may even lead to small, but autonomous *research islands* within the overall research project. For example:

OVERALL RESEARCH PROJECT

Part 1 – Classifying research objective
- Description characteristics (of different legal constructs)
- Comparison (to find similarities and differences)
- Evaluation (to assess which characteristics are met)

Part 2 – Comparative research objective
- Description (foreign legal systems)
- Comparison (foreign legal systems)
- Explanation (of uncovered similarities and differences)
- Evaluation (of results of comparison)

Part 3 – Evaluative research objective
- Describing (case law of different courts)
- Classifying (case law of different courts)
- Theory-building (to uncover underlying principles which can be used as evaluation criteria)

According to our PhD project, these *research islands* have their own unique interaction of research objectives, depending on the specific topic and the needs of the overall research project. The interaction between research objectives was not only an interesting finding, it immediately issued an important methodological warning: because of the indispensable link between the type of research objective and its methodological features, it is important to realize that each research objective involved in the interaction or the research island will have its own methodological features. Legal scholars should keep this in mind when reflecting and deciding on the methodology of their research project.

4 Translation of: "In hetgeen nu volgt zal de houding van de Belgische rechtspraak ten aanzien van het standstillbeginsel worden onderzocht. In chronologische volgorde komt de rechtspraak van de Raad van State, het Hof van Cassatie en het Arbitragehof aan de orde. Hierbij worden naar gelijkenissen en verschillen gezocht, om daarna tot een poging van algemene theorie terzake te komen." G. MAES, *De afdwingbaarheid van sociale grondrechten*, PhD University of Antwerp, 2003.

4.3 RESEARCHER'S FRAME OF REFERENCE

The way in which legal scholars approach and carry out their research is always determined by their *frame of reference.* HUTCHINSON refers to it as a "personal conceptual framework":

> "The conceptual framework includes all this conceptual baggage: a mix of assumptions, experiences, values and beliefs held by the researcher about the topic/ question. The conceptual framework is often the source of interest in the topic and the angle taken by the researcher. Awareness of conceptual baggage, which inevitably exists in any researcher, can provide insight about choice of topic and direction. It can alert a researcher to potential biases. At the same time, conceptual baggage can highlight the strengths and priorities that the researcher is bringing into a project. Instead of pretending it is not there (objectivity), acknowledging conceptual baggage ensures that the researcher is there in the research (subjectively). This process is one step towards developing scholarship, while at the same time avoiding advocacy, no matter how 'well dressed'"[5]

In this section we look into the researcher's frame of reference by clarifying its constituents and by discussing its methodological influence on a research project.

4.3.1 CONSTITUENTS OF THE RESEARCHER'S FRAME OF REFERENCE

A researcher's frame of reference is shaped by different elements and evolves throughout the years. First of all, the researcher's legal education. Organizing a legal education program always presupposes "an (implicit) view on law and legal scholarship."[6] Legal researchers will be influenced by this (implicit) set of legal standards, which were passed on during their education. This means that two legal scholars with a different education background (e.g. different universities or different generations) can sense and deal with the same legal issue in a different way.

Second, the researcher's "world view."[7] This world view consists of personal views on the topics under consideration, on the interests involved, on the organization and functioning of a society, on moral standards and ethical issues,

5 T. HUTCHINSON, *Researching and writing in law,* Sydney, Lawbook Co., 2006, 187.

6 F.B.M. KUNNEMAN, "Object en methoden van rechtswetenschap en juridisch onderwijs" in O.W.M. KAMSTRA, F.B.M. KUNNEMAN and C.W. MARIS (red.), *Nederlandse* rechtswetenschap, Zwolle, W.E.J. Tjeenk Willink, 1988, 173.

7 M. PENDLETON, "Non-empirical Discovery in Legal Scholarship – Choosing, Researching and Writing a Traditional Scholarly Article" in M. MCCONVILLE and W. HONG CHUI (eds.), *Research Methods for Law,* Edinburgh, Edinburgh University Press, 2007, 164–165.

etc.[8] It also includes the researcher's ideological and political beliefs.[9] Legal scholars are sometimes not really aware of their own 'world view'[10], which is, however, very personal and different from that of other researchers.

Finally, the research context. Research schools or departments often have their own and unique academic approach (*wissenschaftliche Richtung*) which is the result of "a common political, ideological, or philosophical background into which a certain theoretical or doctrinal framework is embedded".[11] Moreover, during the research process legal scholars will be significantly influenced by their supervisors and colleagues.[12] This is especially true in the case of individual studies that are components of a large research project. Also external funding agencies imposing clear output goals or editorial boards of scientific journals and publishing houses can leave their mark.[13]

To conclude, the frame of reference of legal scholars is shaped by their legal education and professional experience, their own personal 'world view' and the research context. These three constituents are by nature dynamic and can evolve or change throughout time. Such changes or developments will of course influence the researcher's frame of reference.

4.3.2 METHODOLOGICAL INFLUENCE OF THE RESEARCHER'S FRAME OF REFERENCE

The methodological influence of the researcher's frame of reference is a consequence of the fact that legal scholars do not study law as a distant object or in a laboratory. On the contrary, they are rather close to their research object, as they are actively involved in a legal tradition and a society which is regulated by law. In this respect, we can refer back to FRANKENBERG, who stated in the context of comparative law:

> "instead of pretending to the posture of a neutral, objective, and disinterested observer, the comparatist has to regard herself as being involved: involved in an

---

8 H. TIJSSEN, *De juridische dissertatie onder de loep*, The Hague, Boom Juridische uitgevers, 2009, 154; F. KUNNEMAN, *Rechtswetenschap*, Nijmegen, Ars Aequi Libri, 1991, 9; C.J.J.M. STOLKER, "Ja, geléérd zijn jullie wel!", 2003, https://openaccess.leidenuniv.nl/handle/1887/3727, 9; E.L. RUBIN, "The Practice and Discourse of Legal Scholarship", *Mich.L.Rev.* 1987–88, 1851, 1864 en 1904.

9 R. BIRK, "Labor Law Scholarship in France, Germany, and Italy: some remarks on a difficult question", *Comparative Labor Law & Policy Journal* 2001–2002, 681.

10 J. SINGER, "Normative Methods for Lawyers", *Harvard Law School Public Law Research Paper No. 08-05*, 2008, 55.

11 R. BIRK, "Labor Law Scholarship in France, Germany, and Italy: some remarks on a difficult question", *Comparative Labor Law & Policy Journal* 2001–2002, 698.

12 R. CRYER, T. HERVEY and B. SOKHI-BULLEY, *Research Methodologies in EU and International Law*, Oxford, Hart Publishing, 2011, 31.

13 As regards journals and publishers, see: R. CRYER, T. HERVEY and B. SOKHI-BULLEY, *Research Methodologies in EU and International Law*, Oxford, Hart Publishing, 2011, 31.

> ongoing, particular social practice constituted and pervaded by law; involved in a given legal tradition (a peculiar story of law); and involved in a specific mode of thinking and talking about law."[14]

Legal scholars' frame of reference will significantly influence their methodological choices. A legal scholar, for example, who aims to classify the competences of a judge and who supports a broad interpretation of the assignments/duties of judges will use broader classification criteria than a scholar who interprets the assignments/duties of a judge rather strictly. Or a legal scholar who highly values the connection between law and society will mostly likely prefer a sociological interpretation or an external explanation on the basis of social factors, instead of a grammatical interpretation and an explanation based on an internal approach.

As the frame of reference has an important impact on the research of legal scholars, its influence should be explicit. This does not require that legal scholars have to disclose all their (legal, political, moral, religious and cultural) viewpoints, prejudices and assumptions. It is, however, important to honestly consider personal assumptions, motives and expectations towards the particular topic and the specific research: is it clear for the reader that my project is part of a larger research project focusing on the promotion of European integration? Did I clarify that my theory-building departs from the ECtHR's interpretation of 'positive action' (and not the interpretation according to the CJEU)?

Clarifying these personal assumptions, motives and expectations will make legal scholars more aware of their own prejudices leading to a more transparent research attitude and more attention to counter-arguments. Instead of implicitly postulating assumptions and personal viewpoints as the building blocks of a research, making them explicit will stimulate researchers to look for dissenting authors and contradicting sources. If, for example, legal scholars clarify that their theory-building is based on the ECtHR's interpretation of 'positive action', they are almost automatically incited to clarify that the CJEU has a slightly different interpretation of the same concept.

Moreover, during a research process the knowledge and insights of legal scholars will evolve, influencing their frame of reference. In this respect, some assumptions or expectations at the beginning of a research can be weakened or strengthened by the end of the research. By making them explicit at the beginning, legal scholars will become more aware of changes later on and will be able to reconsider them at the end of the research. The latter will be beneficial to the transparency of the research.

---

14 G. FRANKENBERG, "Critical Comparisons: Re-thinking Comparative Law", *Harv.Int'l L.J.* 1985, 443. See also: J. DE CONINCK, "The Functional Method of Comparative Law: Quo Vadis?", *Rabels Zeitschrift für ausländisches und internationales Privatrecht* 2010, 328 and references.

Finally, knowing the starting points and assumptions of a research is necessary in order to evaluate it. As all legal scholars operate from their own frame of reference, peer reviewers may tend to review someone else's research in view of their own assumptions, viewpoints and expectations regarding the topic and the research project. Although a discussion on (methodological) choices and assumptions is part of the scientific debate, reviewers may never force their own frame of reference to the research of another scholar. In order to avoid this, researchers have the responsibility to inform their readers about the assumptions, personal motives and expectations that are underlying the research project. This way evaluators can take them into account when assessing the research.

5 A PRACTICAL GUIDE ON RESEARCH OBJECTIVES AND METHODOLOGICAL FEATURES

The final part of this handbook translates the theory of the previous parts into a practical guide, which can be used by legal scholars who are designing their own research project. In the first section we bring all the theory of the previous parts together in one overall scheme. This scheme will give a quick and brief overview of the different types of research objectives and their methodological features. It will serve as a practical reminder of the theory discussed.

In the second section we draft a 'list of methodological questions' for each type of research objective. This list is also based on the theory of the previous parts and can be a practical instrument for legal scholars when reflecting on the methodology of their research.

5.1 OVERALL SCHEME

DESCRIPTIVE	CLASSIFYING	COMPARATIVE	THEORY-BUILDING	EXPLANATORY	EVALUATIVE	RECOMMENDATORY
Objective: To systematically analyse a legal construct in all its components in order to present it in an accurate, significant and orderly manner.	**Objective:** To conceptualize or classify (legal) phenomena in the existing legal system	**Objective:** To compare two or more legal constructs/ systems in order to uncover their similarities and differences	**Objective:** To uncover patterns or common denominators from (a set of) legal rules/cases in order to develop a model or theory	**Objective:** To find an explanation for the enactment, alteration, abolishment or current problems of a legal construct	**Objective:** To evaluate a legal construct in view of a norm	**Objective:** To formulate recommendations on how the law *should* be
Methodological features: *Description angle:* – Other research goals? – Which sources are used? *Description structure:* – Existing legal framework – Own structure *Interpretation:* – Types of interpretation:	**Methodological features:** *Classification angle:* – National legal system – International legal community – Other academic disciplines *Classification criteria:* – Existing criteria in legislation, case law or legal doctrine – Own criteria	**Methodological features:** *General features:* – Reason(s) to compare – Micro/macro comparison – *Tertium comparationis* and differences – Choice of legal systems – Access to sources – Comparison approach ▪ Dogmatic ▪ Functional ▪ *Sui generis*	**Methodological features:** *Different types of theories:* – Interpretative – Systematic – Institution – Principle – Fundament *Premises of the theory:* – Internal – External *Abstracting the essence:* – Importance of concepts and classifications	**Methodological features:** *Internal approach:* – Structure/ hierarchy legal system – Preparatory works – Old(er) regulations – Case law – Legal doctrine – Old legal systems *External approach:* – Other academic disciplines	**Methodological features:** *Evaluation criteria:* – Internal criteria – External criteria *Selection criteria:* – Substantive law – Criteria in case law, legislation, legal doctrine, other (legal) documents – Frame of reference *Operationalization:* – Clarify criteria – Concretize (indicators)	**Methodological features:** *Prior description, explanation and evaluation* *Normative criteria:* – Internal – External *Selection criteria:* – Criteria in case law, legislation, legal doctrine, other (legal) documents – Frame of reference

▪ Grammatical ▪ Technical ▪ Systematic ▪ Legal-historical ▪ Teleological ▪ Jurisprudence ▪ Legal doctrine ▪ Non-binding legal sources ▪ Sociological – No hierarchy – Normative choices: ▪ Various/ conflicting possibilities?	*Classification process:* – Describing characteristics of legal constructs and categories involved – Comparing characteristics – Evaluating (in view of classification criteria) under which category a legal construct falls *Classification requirements* – Simple/ unambiguous – Corresponding to reality – Legally functional	*Comparison process:* – Describing legal constructs/systems – Comparing legal constructs/systems – Comparing uncovered similarities and differences – Evaluating results of comparison	*Theory requirements:* – Covering current law and making it more comprehensible – Closed and logical entity – Accurate – Simple, clear and concise conceptual framework *Attention for dissent*		– Reflect on the respective weight of the criteria	*No jump from evaluation to recommendation* *Operationalization:* – Clarify criteria – Concretize criteria (indicators) – Reflect on the respective weight of the criteria *Balancing criteria:* – Internal criteria – External criteria – Results comparison *Types of recommendations:* – Specific – Framework – Facet – Global – Hierarchical – Multiple – Bipartite *Transparent recommendations* – Personal preferences – Attention for dissent

5.2 LIST OF METHODOLOGICAL QUESTIONS

The overall scheme of the previous section serves as a short reminder of the theory explained in part 2 and part 3 of this handbook. In order to increase the practicability of the scheme, we drafted a 'list of methodological questions' for each research objective. We encourage legal scholars to use this list of questions when reflecting on the methodology of their research project.

Descriptive research objective

1. What is my description angle?
   - Did I clarify the sources I used for interpretation?
   - Does the description serve other research goals (e.g. classification, comparison, evaluation etc.)?
2. Which description structure will I use?
   - A structure corresponding to the existing legal framework?
   - A structure proposed by myself?
3. Which different types of interpretation will I use for my description?
   - Grammatical, technical, systematic, legal-historical, teleological, sociological, based on jurisprudence, legal doctrine or non-binding legal sources.
4. Am I aware of the normative choices that I make in case of multiple (contradicting) interpretations?
5. Does my description interact with other research objectives?
   - If so, which research objectives?
   - Can the interaction be considered as an autonomous *research island* within the overall research project?

Classifying research objective

1. What is my classification angle?
2. Which sources will I use for my classification?
   - Sources from a national legal system, from the international legal community, from other academic disciplines?
3. What are my classification criteria?
   - Using existing criteria set forth in legislation, case law and legal doctrine?
   - Proposing my own classification criteria?
4. Do I understand the structure of a classification process?
   - Describing characteristics of legal constructs and categories.
   - Comparing the characteristics.
   - Evaluating (in view of the classification criteria) under which legal category the (legal) phenomenon, which legal constructs belong to same category, etc.
5. Does the classification comply with the following requirements:
   - Simple and unambiguous?
   - Corresponding to reality?
   - Legally functional?
6. Does my classification interact with other research objectives?
   - If so, which research objectives?
   - Can the interaction be considered as an autonomous *research island* within the overall research project?

Comparative research objective

1. Am I pursuing an internal, external or historical comparison? Or a combination?
2. What are my reasons to pursue a comparison?
3. Will my comparison be of a micro or macro nature?
4. Is there a *tertium comparationis* and are there also some differences between the objects of comparison?
5. Which legal constructs/systems do I choose to compare with?
6. Do I have access to sufficient, liable and up-to-date source material?
7. Which approach do I choose for my comparison?
   - Dogmatic, functional, *sui generis*?
8. Do I understand the structure of a comparison process?
   - Describing the legal constructs/systems.
   - Comparing the legal constructs/systems.
   - Explaining uncovered similarities and differences.
   - Evaluating the results of the comparison.
7. Does my comparison interact with other research objectives?
   - If so, which research objectives?
   - Can the interaction be considered as an autonomous *research island* within the overall research project?

Theory-building research objective

1. Which type of theory am I aiming for?
   - Interpretative, systematic, institution, principle, fundament?
2. What are the premises of my theory?
3. Am I aware of the importance of abstraction, concepts and classifications?
4. Does my theory meet the following requirements?
   - Covering current law and making it more comprehensible.
   - Closed and logical entity.
   - Accurate.
   - Simple, clear and using a concise conceptual framework.
5. Did I pay enough attention to dissenting opinions and counter-arguments?
6. Does my theory-building interact with other research objectives?
   - If so, which research objectives?
   - Can the interaction be considered as an autonomous *research island* within the overall research project?

Explanatory research objective

1. Do I choose an internal approach for finding explanations?
   - Structure/hierarchy of the legal system, preparatory works, old(er) regulations, case law, legal doctrine, old legal systems.
2. Do I choose an external approach for finding explanations?
   - Using (knowledge from) other academic disciplines.
3. Does my explanation interact with other research objectives?
   - If so, which research objectives?
   - Can the interaction be considered as an autonomous research island within the overall research project?

Evaluative research objective

1. What are my evaluation criteria?
   - Internal criteria?
   - External criteria?
2. Selecting evaluation criteria:
   - Using existing criteria from legislation, case law, legal doctrine or other (legal) documents?
   - Influence of my frame of reference?
3. Operationalizing evaluation criteria:
   - Clarifying criteria.
   - Concretizing criteria (indicators).
   - Reflecting on the respective weight of the criteria.
4. Does my evaluation interact with other research objectives?
   - If so, which research objectives?
   - Can the interaction be considered as an autonomous research island within the overall research project?

Recommendatory research objective

1. Do I understand the importance of a prior description, explanation and evaluation?
2. What are my normative criteria?
   - Internal
   - External
3. Selecting normative criteria
   - Using existing criteria from legislation, case law, legal doctrine or other (legal) documents?
   - Influence of my frame of reference
4. Operationalizing normative criteria:
   - Clarifying criteria.
   - Concretizing criteria (indicators).
   - Reflecting on the respective weight of the criteria.
5. Am I conscious of the balancing process?
   - Internal criteria, external criteria, results of comparison.
6. What type of recommendation would I like to formulate?
   - Specific, framework, facet, global, hierarchical, multiple, bipartite.
7. Do I formulate recommendations on the basis of their own normative criteria, instead of jumping from the results of an evaluation to a recommendation?
8. Do I clarify my proposed recommendations in a transparent way?
9. Do I pay enough attention to dissenting opinions and counter-arguments?
10. Does the formulation of my recommendations interact with other research objectives?
    - If so, which research objectives?
    - Can the interaction be considered as an autonomous research island within the overall research project?

BIBLIOGRAPHY

AARNIO, A., *Denkweisen der Rechtswissenschaft*, Wien, Springer, 1979, 246 p.

ADAMS, A., "Wat de rechtsvergelijking vermag", *AA* 2011, 192–201.

ADAMS, M., "Controlled Comparison and Language of Description" in ADAMS, M. and HEIRBAUT, D. (eds.), *The Method and Methodology of Comparative Law. Essays in Honour of Mark Van Hoecke*, Oxford, Hart Publishing, 2014, 87–97.

ADAMS, M. and HEIRBAUT, D., "Prolegomena to the Method and Culture of Comparative Law" in ADAMS, M. and HEIRBAUT, D. (eds.), *The Method and Culture of Comparative Law. Essays in Honour of Mark Van Hoecke*, Oxford, Hart Publishing, 2014, 1–21.

ADAMS, M. and BOMHOFF, J. (eds.), *Practice and Theory in Comparative Law*, Cambridge, Cambridge University Press, 2012, 342 p.

ADAMS, M. and GRIFFITHS, J., "Against 'comparative method': explaining similarities and differences" in ADAMS, M. and BOMHOFF, J. (eds.), *Practice and Theory in Comparative Law*, Cambridge, Cambridge University Press, 2012, 279–301.

ADAMS, M., "Doing What Doesn't come Naturally. On the Distinctiveness of Comparative Law" in VAN HOECKE, M. (ed.), *Methodologies of Legal Research*, Oxford, Hart Publishing, 2011, 229–240.

ALEXANDER, L., "What We Do, and Why We Do it", *Stan.L.Rev.* 1993, 1885–1904.

BARENDRECHT, M., VRANKEN, J., GIESEN, I., BORGERS, M.J., VAN DER BRUG, W., TIJSSEN, H.E.B., VAN ROERMUND, G.C.G.J. and VAN BOOM, W.H., "Methoden van rechtswetenschap: komen we verder?", *NJB* 2004, 1419–1428.

BARENDRECHT, M.J., "Rechtswetenschap: stoffig of inventief?", *NJB* 1996, 705–714.

BELL, J., "Legal Research and the Distinctiveness of Comparative Law" in VAN HOECKE, M. (ed.), *Methodologies of Legal Research*, Oxford, Hart Publishing, 2011, 155–176.

BELL, J. and ENGLE, G., *Cross: Statutory Interpretation*, London, Butterworths, 1995, 221 p.

BIRK, R., "Labor Law Scholarship in France, Germany, and Italy: some remarks on a difficult question", *Comparative Labor Law & Policy Journal* 2001–2002, 679–700.

BLOEMBERGEN, A.R., "Iets over object en methode van wetenschap en rechtspraak in het privaatrecht" in KAMSTRA, O.W.M., KUNNEMAN, F.B.M. and MARIS, C.W. (eds.), *Nederlandse rechtswetenschap. Tussen distantie en betrokkenheid: paradigma's in de twintigste eeuw*, Zwolle, W.E.J. Tjeenk Willink, 1988, 61–80.

BREMS, E., "Methods in Legal Human Rights Research" in COOMANS, F., GRÜNFELD, F. and KAMMINGA, T., *Methods of Human Rights Research*, Antwerp, Intersentia, 2009, 77–90.

BRUGGINK, J.J.H., *Wat zegt Scholten over recht*, Zwolle, W.E.J. Tjeenk Willink, 1983, 304 p.

COUNCIL OF AUSTRALIAN LAW DEANS, *Statement on the Nature of Legal Research*, May and October 2005, https://cald.asn.au/wp-content/uploads/2017/11/cald-statement-on-the-nature-of-legal-research-20051.pdf, 7 p.

CRYER, R., HERVEY, T. and SOKHI-BULLEY, B., *Research Methodologies in EU and International Law*, Oxford, Hart Publishing, 2011, 143 p.
CUMYN, M. and SAMSON, M., "La méthodologie juridique en quête d'identité", *RIEJ* 2013, 42 p.
CURRY-SUMNER, I., KIRSTEN, F., VAN DER LINDEN-SMITH, T. and TIGCHELAAR, J., *Onderzoeksvaardigheden*, Nijmegen, Ars Aequi Libri, 2010, 68 p.
DANNEMANN, G., "Comparative Law: Study of Similarities or Differences" in REIMANN, M. and ZIMMERMANN, R. (eds.), *The Oxford Handbook of Comparative Law*, Oxford, Oxford University Press, 2006, 383–418.
DE CONINCK, J., "The Functional Method of Comparative Law: Quo Vadis?", *Rabels Zeitschrift für ausländisches und internationales Privatrecht* 2010, 318–350.
DE GEEST, G., "Hoe maken we van de rechtswetenschap een volwaardige wetenschap?", *NJB* 2004, 58–65.
DE GROOT, G.-R., "Legal Translation" in SMITS, J.M. (ed.), *Elgar Encylcopedia of Comparative Law*, Cheltenham, Edward Elgar, 2006, 423–433.
DELNOY, P., *Eléments de méthodologie juridique*, Brussels, Larcier, 2008, 447 p.
DEVROE, W., *Rechtsvergelijking in een context van europeanisering en globalisering, Leuven*, Acco, 2010, 298 p.
DEVROE, W., *Inleiding tot de rechtsvergelijking*, Leuven, Acco, 2006, 229 p.
DREIER, R., *Recht-Moral-Ideologie*, Frankfurt am Main, Suhrkamp, 1981, 366 p.
EGGERMONT, E., GEUENS, M., GOWIE, F. and TIMBERMONT, E., *Het juridisch verwerkingsproces*, Bruges, die Keure, 2014, 227 p.
EPSTEIN, R.A., "Let 'The Fundamental Things Apply': Necessary and Contingent Truths in Legal Scholarship", *Harv.L.Rev.* 2002, 1288–1313.
FEINMAN, J.M., "The Jurisprudence of Classification", *Stan.L.Rev.* 1989, 661–717.
FELDMAN, D., "The Nature of Legal Scholarship", *The Modern Law Review* 1989, 498–517.
FISHER, E., LANGE, B., SCOTFORD, E. and CARLARNE, C., "Maturity and Methodology: Starting a Debate about Environmental Law Scholarship", *JEL* 2009, 213–250.
FRANKEN, H., *Encyclopedie van de rechtswetenschap*, Deventer, Gouda Quint, 2001, 534 p.
FRANKENBERG, G., "Critical Comparisons: Re-thinking Comparative Law", *Harv.Int'l L.J.* 1985, 411–455.
FRUYTIER, P.A., "Enkele beschouwingen over de interdisciplinaire rechtswetenschap. Braudel als uitgangspunt van een afbakening?", *AA* 2007, 831–836.
GIESEN, I., "The Use and Incorporation of Extralegal Insights in Legal Reasoning", *Utrecht Law Review* 2015, 1–18.
GIESEN, I., "Het incorporeren van extrajuridische inzichten in het privaatrechtelijke debat" in VAN DIJCK, G., VAN GESTEL, R., GIESEN, I. and HAMMERSTEIN, F. (red.), *Cirkels. Een terugblik op een vooruitziende blik*, Deventer, Kluwer, 2013, 217–231.
GOODRICH, P., *Reading the Law. A Critical Introduction to Legal Method and Techniques*, Oxford, Basil Blackwell, 1986, 229 p.
GORLÉ, F., BOURGEOIS, G., BOCKEN, H., REYNTJENS, F., DE BONDT, W. and LEMMENS, K., *Rechtsvergelijking*, Mechelen, Kluwer, 2007, 359 p.
GROENEWEGEN, F.T., *Wetsinterpretatie en rechtsvorming*, The Hague, Boom Juridische uitgevers, 2006, 234 p.

HAENTJENS, R.C.P., HELLINGMAN, C., KAMSTRA, O.W.M., KUNNEMAN, F.B.M. and VERHORST, M., "Object en methode in de Nederlandse rechtswetenschap: op zoek naar standpunten", *NJB* 1985, 806–808.

HAGE, J., "The Method of a Truly Normative Legal Science" in VAN HOECKE, M. (ed.), *Methodologies of Legal Research*, Oxford, Hart Publishing, 2011, 19–44.

HALPÉRIN, J.-L., "Law in books and law in action: the problem of legal change", *Me.L.Rev.* 2011-2012, 46–76.

HERWEIJER, M., "Juridisch onderzoek" in BROEKSTEEG, J.W.L. and STAMHUIS, E.F. (eds.), *Rechtswetenschappelijk onderzoek. Over object en methode*, The Hague, Boom Juridische uitgevers, 2003, 23–33.

HERWEIJER, M., "Normen en rechtshandelingen. Rechtswetenschap als interpreteren en observeren" in BROEKSTEEG, J.W.L. and STAMHUIS, E.F. (eds.), *Rechtswetenschappelijk onderzoek. Over object en methode*, The Hague, Boom Juridische uitgevers, 2003, 53–65.

HESSELINK, M.W., *Contractenrecht in perspectief*, The Hague, Boom Juridische uitgevers, 2004, 223 p.

HILL, J., "Comparative Law, Law Reform and Legal Theory", *O.J.L.S.* 1989, 101–115.

HIRSCH BALLIN, E.M.H., "Object en methode van de wetenschap van het staatsrecht en het bestuursrecht" in KAMSTRA, O.W.M., KUNNEMAN, F.B.M. and MARIS, C.W. (eds.), *Nederlandse rechtswetenschap. Tussen distantie en betrokkenheid: paradigma's in de twingtigste eeuw*, Zwolle, W.E.J. Tjeenk Willink, 1988, 81–99.

HOEKX, N., VANHOVE, K. and VERBEKE, A., "Yes we care! Bedenkingen over de (methode der) rechtswetenschap", *RW* 2008–09, 1785–1789.

HOL, A.M., "Pleidooi voor een jurisprudentia. Over recht en rechtswetenschap" in BROEKSTEEG, J.W.L. and STAMHUIS, E.F. (eds.), *Rechtswetenschappelijk onderzoek. Over object en methode*, The Hague, Boom Juridische uitgevers, 2003, 5–22.

HUSA, J., "Research Designs of Comparative Law – Methodology or Heuristics" in ADAMS, M. and HEIRBAUT, D. (eds.), *The Method and Culture of Comparative Law*, Oxford, Hart Publishing, 2014, 53–68.

HUSA, J., "Comparative Law, Legal Linguistics and Methodology of Legal Doctrine" in VAN HOECKE, M. (ed.), *Methodologies of Legal Research*, Oxford, Hart Publishing, 2011, 209–228.

HUSA, J., "Farewell to Functionalism of Methodological Tolerance?", *The Rabel Journal of Comparative and International Private Law* 2003, 419–447.

HUTCHINSON, T., *Researching and writing in law*, Sydney, Lawbook Co., 2010, 461 p.

HUTCHINSON, T., "Doctrinal research" in WATKINS, D. and BURTON, M. (eds.), *Research Methods in Law*, London, Routledge, 2013, 7–33.

HUTCHINSON, T. and DUNCAN, N., "Defining and Describing What We Do: Doctrinal Legal Research", *Deakin LR* 2012, 82–119.

JANSEN, N., "Comparative Law and Comparative Knowledge" in REIMANN, M. and ZIMMERMANN, R. (eds.), *The Oxford Handbook of Comparative Law*, Oxford, Oxford University Press, 2006, 306–338.

JOLOWICZ, H.F., *Lectures on Jurisprudence*, London, Athlone Press, 1963, 391 p.

KAMPHUISEN, P.W., *Beschouwingen over rechtswetenschap*, Nijmegen, Dekker & Van De Vegt, 1938, 127 p.

KAMSTRA, O.W.M., KUNNEMAN, F.B.M. and MARIS, C.W., (eds.), *Nederlandse rechtswetenschap. Tussen distantie en betrokkenheid: paradigma's in de twintigste eeuw*, Zwolle, W.E.J. Tjeenk Willink, 1988, 361 p.

KANTOROWICZ, H.U. and PATTERSON, E.W., "Legal Science - A Summary of Its Methodology", *Colum.L.Rev.* 1928, 679–707.

KESTEMONT, L., "A Meta-Methodological Study of Dutch and Belgian PhDs on Social Security Law: Devising a Typology Of Research Objectives as a Supporting Tool", *E.J.S.S.* 2015, 361–384.

KESTEMONT, L., Naar een rechtswetenschappelijke methodeleer. Een expliciet methodologisch kader voor rechtswetenschappelijk onderzoek in het socialezekerheidsrecht, Bruges, die Keure, 2017, 335 p.

KESTEMONT, L., *Ockhams scheermes in het leerstuk van de Belgische nalatigheidsinteresten*, Bruges, die Keure, 2012, 158 p.

KISSAM, P.C., "The evaluation of legal scholarship", *Wash.L.Rev.* 1998, 221–255.

KORREL, P.G. and KAMSTRA, O.W.M., *Sociaal wetenschappelijke & juridische methodologie*, Amsterdam, Melkman, 1991, 343 p.

KRANENBURG, R., *De grondslagen der rechtswetenschap*, Haarlem, Tjeenk Willink, 1952, 183 p.

KUNNEMAN, F., *Rechtswetenschap*, Nijmegen, Ars Aequi Libri, 1991, 63 p.

KUNNEMAN, F.B.M., "Object en methoden van rechtswetenschap en juridisch onderwijs" in KAMSTRA, O.W.M., KUNNEMAN, F.B.M. and MARIS, C.W. (eds.), *Nederlandse rechtswetenschap. Tussen distantie en betrokkenheid: paradigma's in de twingtigste eeuw*, Zwolle, W.E.J. Tjeenk Willink, 1988, 173–191.

KUNNEMAN, F., *Over het inleiden tot de rechtswetenschap*, Delft, Eburon, 1986, 194 p.

LARENZ, K., *Methodenlehre der Rechtswissenschaft*, Berlin, Springer, 1983, 483 p.

LANGEMEIJER, G.E., "Recht en Rechtsbeschouwing in de tweede helft van de Twintigste Eeuw" in POLAK, J.M., *Vooruitzichten van de Rechtswetenschap*, Deventer, Kluwer, 1964, 1–29.

LEEUW, F.L., "Empirical Legal Research: The Gap between Facts and Values and Legal Academic Training", *Utrecht Law Review* 2015, 19–33.

LEMMENS, K., "Comparative law as an act of modesty: a pragmatic and realistic approach to comparative legal scholarship" in ADAMS, M. and BOMHOFF, J. (eds.), *Practice and Theory in Comparative Law*, Cambridge, Cambridge University Press, 2012, 302–324.

LÖHNIG, M., "A Few Words about Comparative Legal History" in ADAMS, M. and HEIRBAUT, D. (eds.), *The Method and Culture of Comparative Law*, Oxford, Hart Publishing, 2014, 113–120.

MACCORMICK, N., *Rhetoric and the Rule of Law*, Oxford, Oxford University Press, 2005, 287 p.

MACCORMICK, D.N. and SUMMERS, R.S. (eds.), *Interpreting Statutes*, Aldershot, Dartmouth, 1991, 567 p.

MACCORMICK, D.N. and SUMMERS, R.S., "Interpretation and Justification" in MACCORMICK, D.N. and SUMMERS, R.S. (eds.), *Interpreting Statutes*, Aldershot, Dartmouth, 1991, 511–544.

MACKOR, A.R., "Legal Doctrine As a Non-Normative Discipline", *ReM* 2012, afl. 1, 22–45.

MARIS, C.W., "Distantie en betrokkenheid in de rechtswetenschap" in KAMSTRA, O.W.M., KUNNEMAN, F.B.M. and MARIS, C.W. (eds.), *Nederlandse rechtswetenschap. Tussen distantie en betrokkenheid: paradigma's in de twingtigste eeuw*, Zwolle, W.E.J. Tjeenk Willink, 1988, 3–38.

MCCONVILLE, M. and HONG CHUI, W., (eds.), *Research Methods for Law*, Edinburgh, Edinburgh University Press, 2007, 239 p.

MCCRUDDEN, C., "Legal Research and the Social Sciences", *L.Q.R.* 2006, 632–650.

MEIJERS, E.M., *Dogmatische rechtswetenschap*, 's-Gravenhage, Belinfante, 1903, 203 p.

MICHAELS, R., "The Functional Method of Comparative Law" in REIMANN, M. and ZIMMERMANN, R. (eds.), *The Oxford Handbook of Comparative Law*, Oxford, Oxford University Press, 2006, 339–382.

MORRIS, C. and MURPHY, C., *Getting a PhD in Law*, Oxford, Hart Publishing, 2011, 158 p.

NEERGAARD, U., NIELSEN, R. and ROSEBERRY, L. (eds.), *European Legal Method – Paradoxes and Revitalisation*, Kopenhagen, DJØF Publishing, 2011, 378 p.

NERHOT, P., "Interpretation in Legal Science" in NERHOT, P. (ed.), *Law, Interpretation and Reality*, Dordrecht, Kluwer, 1990, 191–225.

ODERKERK, A.E., *De preliminaire fase van het rechtsvergelijkend onderzoek*, Nijmegen, Ars Aequi Libri, 1999, 484 p.

OOST, H., BREKELMANS, M., SWANBORN, P. and WESTHOFF, G., "Naar een didactiek van de probleemstelling", *Pedagogische Studiën Jaargang* 2002, 18–36 en www.phdcentre.eu/nl/publicaties/documents/DidactiekvdProbleemstellingOost e.a.2002.pdf, 27 p.

OOST, H., *Circling Around a Question: Defining Your Research Problem*, Utrecht, IVLOS, 2003, 34.

OOST, H.A., *De kwaliteit van probleemstellingen in dissertaties*, Utrecht, Elinkwijk, 1999, 305 p.

OOST, H.A., *Hoe schrijf ik een betere scriptie. Een nieuwe methode voor het schrijven van scripties en andere teksten*, Amsterdam, Contact, 1995, 141 p.

OOST, H. and MARKENHOFF, A., *Een onderzoek voorbereiden*, Baarn, HB-uitgevers, 2007, 79 p.

ÖRÜCÜ, E., "Developing Comparative Law" in ÖRÜCÜ, E. and NELKEN, D. (eds.), *Comparative Law*, Oxford, Hart Publishing, 2007, 43–65.

PATTERSON, B.L., THORNE, S.E., CANAM C., and JILLINGS C., *Meta-Study of Qualitative Health Research*, Thousand Oaks, Sage, 2001, 162 p.

PECZENIK, A., "Scientia Juris. Legal Doctrine as knowledge of Law and as a Source of Law" in PATTARO, E. (ed.), *A Treatise of Legal Philosophy and General Jurisprudence*, Dordrecht, Springer, 2005, 180 p.

PECZENIK, A., *On Law and Reason*, Dordrecht, Kluwer, 1989, 443 p.

PENDLETON, M., "Non-empirical Discovery in Legal Scholarship – Choosing, Researching and Writing a Traditional Scholarly Article" in MCCONVILLE, M. and HONG CHUI, W. (eds.), *Research Methods for Law*, Edinburgh, Edinburgh University Press, 2007, 159–180.

PIETERS, D., "Functions of comparative law and practical methodology of comparing" in *Syllabus Research Master in Law*, Leuven-Tilburg, 2009, 35 p.

PIETERS, D., "Reflections on the methodology of social security law comparison" in GREVE, B. and PIETERS, D. (eds.), *Social security in an interdisciplinary perspective*, Antwerp, Maklu, 1999, 103–112.

PIETERS, D., *Sociale-zekerheidsrechtsvergelijking ten dienste van Europa*, Deventer, Kluwer, 1992, 79 p.

PIMONT, S., "À propos de l'activité doctrinale civiliste", *RTDCiv.* 2006, 707–718.

PINTENS, W., *Inleiding tot de rechtsvergelijking*, Leuven, Universitaire Pers Leuven, 1998, 265 p.

POLAK, J.M., *Theorie en practijk der rechtsvinding*, Zwolle, W.E.J. Tjeenk Willink, 1953, 86 p.

POSNER, R.A., "Legal Scholarship Today", *Harv.L.Rev.* 2002, 1314–1326.

REITZ, J.C., "How to Do Comparative Law?", *Am.J.Comp.L.* 1998, 617–636.

ROUX, T.R., "Judging the quality of legal research: A qualified response to the demand for greater methodological rigour", *SSRN* 2014, 20 p.

ROUX, T.R., "The Incorporation Problem in Interdisciplinary Legal Research: Some Conceptual Issues and a Practical Illustration", *SSRN* 2014, 14 p.

RUBIN, E.L., "Law and the Methodology of Law", *Wis.L.Rev.* 1997, 521–565.

RUBIN, E.L., "The Practice and Discourse of Legal Scholarship", *Mich.L.Rev.* 1987–88, 1835–1905.

SALTER, M. and MASON, J., *Writing Law Dissertations*, Essex, Pearson, 2007, 245 p.

SAMUEL, G., "Does One Need an Understanding of Methodology in Law Before One Can Understand Methodology in Comparative Law" in VAN HOECKE, M. (ed.), *Methodologies of Legal Research, Oxford,* Hart Publishing, 2011, 177–208.

SAMUEL, G., *Epistemology and Method in Law*, Aldershot, Ashgate, 2003, 384 p.

SCHLAG, P., "Spam Jurisprudence, Air Law, and the Rank of Anxiety of Nothing Happening, *Geo.L.J.* 2009, 803–835.

SCHMITTHOFF, M., "The science of comparative law", *C.L.J.* 1939, 94–110.

SCHOLTEN, P., "Algemeen Deel" in *Asser's Handleiding tot de beoefening van het Nederlandsch Burgerlijk Recht*, Zwolle, W.E.J. Tjeenk Willink, 1954, 251 p.

SCHOLTEN, P., "De structuur der rechtswetenschap" in *Verzamelde Geschriften van wijlen Prof. Mr. Paul Scholten*, Zwolle, Tjeenk Willink, 1949, 521 p.

SIEBURGH, C.H., "L'art de la distinction", *NJB* 2008, 3–13.

SIEMS, M., *Comparative Law*, Cambridge, Cambridge University Press, 2014, 416 p.

SIEMS, M.M., "The Curious Case of Overfitting Legal Transplants," in ADAMS, M. and HEIRBAUT, D. (eds.), *The Method and Culture of Comparative Law*, Oxford, Hart Publishing, 2014, 133–146.

SIEMS, M.M., "A World without Law Professors" in VAN HOECKE, M. (ed.), *Methodologies of Legal Research*, Oxford, Hart Publishing, 2011, 75.

SIEMS, M.M., "Legal Originality", *O.J.L.S.* 2008, 147–164.

SINGER, J., "Normative Methods for Lawyers", *Harvard Law School Public Law Research Paper* No. 08–05, 2008, 92 p.

SMITH, C., Het normatieve karakter van de rechtswetenschap: recht als oordeel", *R & R* 2009, 202–225.

SMITH, C.E., GEELHOED, W., DUBELAAR, M.J., TER HAAR, B.P., VAN RIJN VAN ALKEMADE, J., VAN WILLIGENBURG, K., SPRANGERS, A., VAN RIJN, J., ELSEMAN, T., BOGAERTS, A., DE GOEDE, S., ALSEMGEEST, J.,

BOGAERTS, A., KOUSEDGHI, S., and VAN DER DEIJL, E., "Criteria voor goed rechtswetenschappelijk onderzoek. De omgekeerde route", *NJB* 2008, 685–690.

SMITS. J., "Law and Interdisciplinarity: On the Inevitable Normativity of Legal Studies", *Critical Analysis of Law* 2014, 5–86.

SMITS, J., *Omstreden Rechtswetenschap: over aard, methode en organisatie van de juridische discipline*, The Hague, Boom Juridische uitgevers, 2009, 235 p.

SMITS, J.M., *The Mind and Method of the Legal Academic*, Cheltenham, Edward Elgar, 2012, 180 p.

SNEL, M.V.R., "Source-usage within doctrinal legal inquiry: choices, problems, and challenges", *ReM* 2014, afl. 3, 21 p.

SOETEMAN, A., "Wetenschappelijke rechtsgeleerdheid", *R & R* 2009, 226–235.

STEINER, E., *French Legal Method*, Oxford, Oxford University Press, 2002, 241 p.

STOLKER, C., *Rethinking The Law School. Education, Research, Outreach and Governance,* Cambridge, Cambridge University Press, 2014, 472 p.

STOLKER, C., "Een discipline in transitie, *ReM* 2011, afl. 1, 13–43.

STOLKER, C.J.J.M., "Wat maakt een juridisch tijdschrift wetenschappelijk?, *NJB* 2004, 1409–1418.

STOLKER, C.J.J.M., "Ja, geléérd zijn jullie wel!", *NJB* 2003, 1409–1418 en https://openaccess.leidenuniv.nl/handle/1887/3727, 20 p.

STONE, F.F., "The end to be served by comparative law", *Tul.L.Rev.* 1950–51, 325–335.

SUMMERS, R.S. and TARUFFO, M., "Interpretation and Comparative Analysis" in MACCORMICK, D.N. and SUMMERS, R.S., (eds.), *Interpreting Statutes*, Aldershot, Dartmouth, 1991, 461–510.

TAEKEMA, S. and VAN KLINK, B., "On the Border. Limits and Possibilities of Interdisciplinary Research" in TAEKEMA, S. and VAN KLINK, B. (eds.), *Law and Method*, Tübingen, Mohr Siebeck, 2011, 7–32.

TANQUEREL, T. and FLÜKIGER, A. (eds.), *L'évaluation de la recherche en droit. Enjeux et méthodes*, Brussels, Bruylant, 2015, 488 p.

TIJSSEN, H., *De juridische dissertatie onder de loep*, The Hague, Boom Juridische uitgevers, 2009, 252 p.

TJONG TJIN TAI, T.F.E., "Verantwoording van bronnen" in VAN DIJCK, G., VAN GESTEL, R., GIESEN, I. and HAMMERSTEIN, F. (red.), *Cirkels. Een terugblik op een vooruitziende blik*, Deventer, Kluwer, 2013, 201–208.

TWINING, W., FARNSWORTH, W., VOGENAUER, S., en TESÓN, F., "The role of the academics in the legal system" in P. CANE and M. TUSHNET (eds.), *The Oxford Handbook of Legal Studies*, Oxford, Oxford University Press, 2003, 920–949.

TWINING,W., *Law in context*, Oxford, Clarendon Press, 1997, 365 p.

VALCKE, C. en GRELLETTE, M., "Three Functions of Function in Comparative Legal Studies" in ADAMS, M. and HEIRBAUT, D. (eds.), *The Method and Culture of Comparative Law*, Oxford, Hart Publishing, 2014, 99–111.

VALCKE, C., "Reflections on comparative law methodology – getting inside contract law" in ADAMS, M. and BOMHOFF, J. (eds.), *Practice and Theory in Comparative Law*, Cambridge, Cambridge University Press, 2012, 22–48.

VAN BEMMELEN, P., *Regtsgeleerde opstellen*, I, Leiden, E.J. Brill, 1891, 436 p.

VAN BOOM, W. and VAN GESTEL, R., "Rechtswetenschappelijk onderzoek. Een samenvatting van de uitkomsten van een landelijke enquête", *NJB* 2015, (full version available online), 38 p.

VAN BOOM, W.H., "Empirisch privaatrecht: enige beschouwingen over de rol van empirisch onderzoek in de hedendaagse privaatrechtswetenschap", *TPR* 2013, 1–84.

VAN DAMME, E. "Verwevenheid van recht en economie" in GROENHUIJSEN, M., HONDIUS, E. and SOETEMAN, A. (eds.), *Recht in Geding*, The Hague, Boom Juridische Uitgeverij, 2014, 259–296.

VAN DIJCK, G., *Kwaliteit van de juridische annotatie*, The Hague, Boom Juridische uitgevers, 2011, 170 p.

VANGEEBERGEN, B. and VAN DAELE, D., "Is de studie van het recht een wetenschap en wie kan het wat schelen?, *RW* 2009, 986–994.

VAN GESTEL, R., "Evaluating Legal Research: About the Good, the Bad, and the Ugly" in TANQUEREL, T. and FLÜKIGER, A. (eds.), *L'évaluation de la recherche en droit. Enjeux et méthodes*, Brussels, Bruylant, 2015, 27–55.

VAN GESTEL, R.A.J., Preadvies "Kwaliteit van juridische publicaties. Over ranking, peer review, sciëntometrics en vertrouwen in alternatieve evaluatiemethoden" in HANDELINGEN NEDERLANDSE JURISTEN-VERENIGING, *Kwaliteit als keuze in rechtspraak, wetgeving en rechtswetenschap*, Deventer, Kluwer, 2015, 243–378.

VAN GESTEL, R., MICKLITZ, H.-W. and POIARES MADURO, M., "Methodology in the New Legal World", *Department of Law EUI Working Papers*, 2012/13, 23 p.

VAN GESTEL, R. en MICKLITZ, H.-W., "Revitalising Doctrinal Legal Research in Europe: What About Methodology?" in NEERGAARD, U., NIELSEN, R. and ROSEBERRY, L. (eds.), *European Legal Method – Paradoxes and Revitalisation*, Kopenhagen, DJØF Publishing, 2011, 25–73.

VAN GESTEL, R. and VRANKEN, J., "Assessing Legal Research: Sense and Nonsense of Peer Review versus Bibliometrics and the Need for a European Approach, *German Law Journal* 2011, 901–929.

VAN GESTEL, R.A.J. and VRANKEN, J.B.M., "Rechtswetenschappelijke artikelen", *NJB* 2007, 1448–1461.

VAN HOECKE, M., "De evaluatie van rechtswetenschappelijk onderzoek", *RW* 2015, 123–140.

VAN HOECKE, M., "Preface" in VAN HOECKE, M. (ed.), *Methodologies of Legal Research*, Oxford, Hart Publishing, 2011, iii-ix.

VAN HOECKE, M. (ed.), *Methodologies of Legal Research*, Oxford, Hart Publishing, 2011, 294 p.

VAN HOECKE, M., "Legal Doctrine: Which Method(s) for What Kind of Discipline?" in VAN HOECKE, M. (ed.), *Methodologies of Legal Research*, Oxford, Hart Publishing, 2011, 1–18.

VAN HOECKE, M., *Is de rechtswetenschap een empirische wetenschap?*, The Hague, Boom Juridische uitgevers, 2010, 46 p.

VAN HOECKE, M., "Hoe wetenschappelijk is de rechtswetenschap?", *TPR* 2009, 629–688.

VAN HOECKE, M., "Deep Level Comparative Law" in VAN HOECKE, M. (ed.), *Epistemology and Methodology of Comparative Law*, Oxford, Hart, 2004, 398 p.

VAN HOECKE, M., *Inleiding tot het recht. Rechtstheorie. Deel 2*, Brussels, UFSAL Brussel, 1988, 144–294.

VAN HOECKE, M., "Aard en methode van de rechtsdogmatiek", *R & R* 1984, 188–205.
VAN HOECKE, M., *De interpretatievrijheid van de rechter*, Antwerp, Kluwer, 1979, 432 p.
VAN KLINK, B.M.J. and POORT, L.M., "De normativiteit van de rechtswetenschap", *RM Themis* 2013, 258–268.
VAN QUICKENBORNE, M., "Rechtsstudie als wetenschap" in *Actori incumbit probatio. Opstellen aangeboden ter gelegenheid van de eerst promotie rechten aan de universitaire instelling Antwerpen*, Antwerp, Kluwer, 1975, 223–235.
VAN SCHAAIJK, G., "Praktijkgericht juridisch onderzoek", *ReM* 2011, afl. 1, 85–107.
VAN SCHAAIJK, G.A.F.M., Praktijkgericht juridisch onderzoek, The Hague, Boom Juridische uitgevers, 2011, 266 p.
VERHORST, M., "De rechtswetenschappelijke gemeenschap" in KAMSTRA, O.W.M., KUNNEMAN, F.B.M. and MARIS, C.W. (eds.), *Nederlandse rechtswetenschap. Tussen distantie en betrokkenheid: paradigma's in de twingtigste eeuw*, Zwolle, W.E.J. Tjeenk Willink, 1988, 341–358.
VICK, D.W., "Interdisciplinarity and the Discipline of Law", *Brit.J.Law & Soc.* 2004,163–193.
VLIR KWALITEITSZORG ONDERZOEK RECHTEN, *Model voor Integrale Kwaliteitsevaluatie van het Onderzoek in de Rechtswetenschappen*, versie 22 september 2004, www.vlir.be/media/docs/Onderzoeksbeleid/notitie_KZR_22sept2004.pdf, 28 p.
VOGENAUER, S., "Sources of Law and Legal Method in Comparative Law" in REIMANN, M. and ZIMMERMANN, R. (eds.), *The Oxford Handbook of Comparative Law*, Oxford, Oxford University Press, 2006, 869–898.
VRANKEN, J.B.M., "Algemeen Deel. Een synthese" in *Mr. C. Assers Handleiding tot de beoefening van het Nederlands Burgerlijk Recht*, Deventer, Kluwer, 2014, 234 p.
VRANKEN, J., "Wij weten wel wat wij doen. Over juridisch-dogmatisch onderzoek in het privaatrecht, maar wel een slag anders", *NJB* 2014, 1728–1737.
VRANKEN, J.B.M., "Een nieuw rechtsrealisme in het privaatrecht", *WPNR* 2011, 1113–1122.
VRANKEN, J.B.M., "Nieuwe richtingen in de rechtswetenschap, *WPNR* 2010, 318–329.
VRANKEN, J.B.M., "Als een arrest niet bevalt, laten wij het gewoon weg" in NIEUWENHUIS, H. (ed.), *Ex Libris*, Deventer, Kluwer, 2009, 77–94.
VRANKEN, J.B.M., "Algemeen Deel" in *Asser's Handleiding tot de beoefening van het Nederlands Burgerlijk Recht*, Zwolle, W.E.J. Tjeenk Willink, 1995, 94.
WATKINS, D. and BURTON, M. (eds.), *Research Methods in Law*, London, Routledge, 2013, 156 p.
WATSON, A., *Legal Transplants*, Edinburgh, Scottish Academic Press, 1974, 106 p.
WESTERMAN, P.C., "Open or Autonomous? The Debate on Legal Methodology as a Reflection of the Debate on Law" in VAN HOECKE, M. (ed.), *Methodologies of Legal Research*, Oxford, Hart Publishing, 2011, 87–110.
WESTERMAN, P. and WISSINK, M., "Rechtsgeleerdheid als rechtswetenschap", *NJB* 2008, 503–507.
WISSINK, M.H., "Op weg naar een nieuwe ronde", *NJB* 2006, 1360–1365.
ZWEIGERT, K. and KÖTZ, H., *An Introduction to Comparative Law*, Oxford, Oxford University Press, 1997, 744 p.

www.ingramcontent.com/pod-product-compliance
Ingram Content Group UK Ltd.
Pitfield, Milton Keynes, MK11 3LW, UK
UKHW051923100926
8556IPUK00021B/1337

9 781780 686738